BÉLA BARTÓK

HIS LIFE IN PICTURES AND DOCUMENTS

BÉLA BARTÓK

His Life in Pictures and
Documents
by
Ferenc Bónis

BELWIN MILLS PUBLISHING CORPORATION
NEW YORK

Title of the original: Bartók Béla élete képekben és dokumentumokban, Zeneműkiadó, 1972
First published in the United States of America in 1972
by Belwin Mills Publishing Corporation, New York, N.Y. 11571
Translated by Lili Halápy. Translation revised by Kenneth McRobbie. Binding and jacket by Klára Rudas.
The photograph on the jacket is by Kata Kálmán

In co-production with Corvina Press, Budapest, with the assistance of Editio Musica Budapest
Library of Congress Catalog Card Number 72–86092
Printed and bound in Hungary, 1972 — Kossuth Printing House, Budapest

To Bence Szabolcsi

The decades since Bartók's death have abundantly confirmed that the œuvre has survived its creator. However, one may say of him what can be said only of few great masters in the history of music: that his human features do not fade with the passing years. On the contrary, the farther the distance from which one looks back upon his career, the clearer and more distinct appears its portrait in ever greater and more subtle detail.

No doubt, a great part of this may be due to international Bartók research. We know more and more of the sources of his art, of the internal ordering of his workshop, which had not been at all obvious in the composer's lifetime. Before long we shall doubtless have reliable information on virtually all aspects of his life, on practically every day of his sixty-four and one half years. By and by the mass of information becomes arranged into a chain of connections, logically motivating and explaining Bartók's actions, his decisions and his different forms of expression.

On the other hand, this large-scale research work itself is rather the consequence of than the ultimate reason for the growing Bartók cult of our time. The roots lie deeper: more and more people are coming to understand his compositions, the *singular* works and also the *general* message of the whole œuvre; more and more recognize in his music their own feelings, desires and fears, their unuttered thoughts. And there are more and more people who want to know *everything* about the artist who created these works.

Everything capable of being expressed in words they want to know in the original and exactly. Because since Bartók's early years the romantic approach to artists and the romantic biographies of artists have been on the wane. Whoever has journeyed with him through heaven and hell, experienced with him all the tortures of his age, and has learned from him to have faith in the future can hardly enjoy the artificially coloured, rapid "literary" representations of the genuine dramas of life. The same anti-romantic forces that have brought into being the new music of our time have made the reader aware of the fact that there is no more exciting experience than truth, the world of facts. This requirement has created a characteristic genre of reading matter which gains increasing significance in our day; this may be termed *literary documentation*, in which scholarly completeness and exactness are blended with an artistic sense of selection and shaping.

However, apart from this general requirement of our period, it would in no way be possible to present a portrait of Béla Bartók without responding to an inner imperative to seek out and manifest truth beyond the limits of style. Of this he himself provided an example through his life and work, virtual incarnations of truth and passionately severe objectivity. When giving the title "The Indivisible Man" to an article on Bartók, Béla Balázs—the eminent poet and aesthete, a contemporary of the composer's and librettist of his two works for the stage—indeed chose the most appropriate of terms.

By means of some one hundred pictures we are going both to document and to conjure up the career of this indivisible man, this epoch-making artist and scholar, whose character was as hard as a diamond. It will be as though the separate frames of a film were projected on the screen of our imagination: in which appear the little boy of five (born in Nagyszentmiklós [now Sînnicolau Mare, Rumania] on the 25th of March, 1881), the grammar-school pupil, the student at the Budapest Academy of Music, the young composer, the world-famous globe-trotting artist in the prime of life and at the zenith of his career, and finally the old man enfeebled and reduced to virtual incorporeality, struggling with a mortal disease and yet with the fire of the spirit in his eyes almost to the end (dying in New York on the 26th of September, 1945). Thus our pictures trace Bartók's career during some six decades, attempting to create a single, summarizing *general* portrait out of its singular components.

What do these "external" and "internal" likenesses represent? The external one is of a body small in frame and well-proportioned in its parts, over which reigns a majestic head. There a lofty brow, a straight nose and firm lips reveal a strong will and but seldom a smile. The "focus" of this portrait is the dark-brown pair of eyes, expressing at times quiet seriousness and interest, at others looking into infinite distances—but most often, bearing witness to stark inner tension, scrutinizing us with a penetrating, glowing radiance. A single glance at his strong and muscular hands will reveal a lot about Bartók the pianist, his steely touch and inexorable rhythm releasing gigantic spiritual energies.

"There was a rhythmical, purposeful sway in his gait," writes Bence Szabolcsi, his contemporary and follower, author of the first Hungarian scholarly biography of Bartók of the highest standards. "The way he threw back his head expressed forcefulness. Those who saw him playing the piano will remember that in his movements, his stretchings and sudden starts there was something of the panther, predacious and fearful."

The reminiscences of Antal Molnár—another Hungarian follower, a collaborator of Bartók and the author of the first published analysis of his works—do but confirm and highlight these traits: "The master's movements are not slow or measured, nor are they sudden, abrupt or over-enthusiastic. They are guided by the golden mean, by cultured self-discipline. During conversation, Bartók does not make a single gesture that would indicate to the listener what kind of man he is confronted with. His every movement is simple, natural, economical, and purposeful; these movements belong harmonically to his 'neutral' exterior. It was as if, instinctively, he exerted the least possible strength to achieve the desired physical results; no trace of any exaggeration, of anything additional intended to suggest or to inspire. In vain would you look for the opposite either: for some intentional suppression or reticence. No, the whole phenomenon gives a wholly natural impression. And it makes an awkward impression only because you *know* that this outward manner does not tally at all with the personality. Never would anybody imagine that the man creating *such* things is *like this*!" It is by sketching in pertinent features that Molnár completes the portrait of Bartók the pianist, too: "...he approaches the instrument with deliberation and a somewhat rolling gait. He sits down to it in the usual way and calmly extends his hands on the keyboard. From the moment he starts playing he seems to be transformed. All his muscles swing into motion, as if, under the effect of some demonic power, his whole being were discharging electricity... Only the player's face remains all the time neutral and pale. But there is a brilliant flash in his eyes, signalling that here he is in his element. Then the waves die down, the tempest abates, the composition is over; the audience, absorbed in its ecstasy, comes to only some moments later to break out in applause showing violent emotion. By then he is standing before them again with his emotionless exterior, without any sign of his calling; the 'clerk', head-nodding his reluctant thanks for the ovation, leaves the platform with the same cautious steps with which he had occupied it. There is not a trace of any excitement or emotion; he is totally lacking the juggler's smile of self-complacency or of gratitude." And how did he play his own works? We may quote Antal Molnár again: "At such times discipline and impetuosity, objectiveness and ecstasy were united in his peerlessly individual way of playing. As though a shower of sparks had been emitted by his ascetic body, as if his muscles had been tightened by gigantic springs—possessed by some magical demonism—he entranced his audience with the instrument. At such times it was primeval nature conveying through him its commands to a new culture."

To emphasize Antal Molnár's affirmation just cited above—"Never would anybody imagine that the man creating *such* things is *like this*"—it may be worth while to insert some observations of Béla Bartók Junior, the composer's elder son, on his father's habits at home. "In his dressing he was simple and unassuming; he could take extraordinary care of his suits, which he kept in a good state for decades. He did not have any special interest in food, but to have meals prepared carefully and absolutely hygienically was essential for him. In general he ate rather little; he took practically no alcohol throughout his life. He had not smoked for a long time: it was only during the First World War that he took it up... He did not go in for any entertainment in the common meaning of the word, that is to say, he did not go to the theatre, cinema, restaurants or other places of amusement; even to concerts he went only rather seldom... Though he never subscribed to any one newspaper he regularly read them and bought one almost every day, and even more than one. He was virtually interested in everything in the papers, in the leaders as well as in the news on economics, politics or the arts. With strangers or those he did not know his manner was always reticent and somewhat cautious, on account of the inclination of people to be obtrusive. But with members of his family and with those he appreciated or had grown fond of his manner was absolutely spontaneous for he liked such company... Because of his reticent demeanour outsiders considered my father austere and even gloomy, although he had a well-developed sense of humour; he liked farcical situations, he liked riddles and puzzles. It is characteristic of his sense of humour that he arranged a fine collection of envelopes with erroneous addresses from his foreign correspondents. For this he had ample opportunities because, in addition to his address at the Academy of Music on Liszt Ferenc Square, all our flats in Budapest were in streets with double consonants in their spelling (Gyopár, Kavics and Csalán Streets, and Szilágyi Dezső Square), which foreigners wrote with the most amusing mistakes. He enjoyed showing them around." Antal Molnár's words counterpoint with the son's recollections: "His joking was rather simple and childish and occurred only in intimate gatherings."

Proceeding along the lines of this "external" portrait, our "internal portrait" of the features of Bartók's character are revealed as it were of their own accord. Zoltán Kodály was his only close friend, and was one of the few people who really knew him. He tried to define Bartók's mentality by means of the types of Kretschmer's characterology, soon after the death of his comrade. "None of the *cyclothymic* features refers to him. Those of the other *(schizothymic)* group do fit: fragile, fine, sensitive, cool, severe, rigid, cold, dull, indolent. (Degrees from the upper extreme to the lower.) All attributes fit him up to the term cold. Also the categories of spiritual tension (starting from the bottom): fanatical, pedantic, persistent, systematic. Only the upper extremes—capricious, confused—do not fit, whereas the others are perfectly appropriate. On agility, speed of stimulus reaction: inadequate; that is to say, stimulus reaction was faster than was normal. The subheadings of this are: restless, flustered, hesitating, gauche, aristocratic, contrived, angular, rigid. With the exception of the last all the others more or less fit him. With respect to social relations: secluded, reserved. Degrees: idealist, reformer, revolutionary, systematic, organizer, self-willed, crotchety, dissatisfied, reticent, suspectful, lonely, unsociable, misanthropic, brutal, anti-social. With the exception of the last three there is none that could not be applied to him more or less with justification. Categories of psychic tension: ingenious, lively, susceptible, energetic, inhibited. He could be a typical instance of the schizothymic frame of mind."

Of course, Kodály added by way of concluding this rather sombre enumeration, "a man is not so simple a thing that his eternal mystery could be solved by a couple of lines on a label..." To understand the changes and development of character, he stated, the effects and modifications occasioned by the circumstances of life should also be scrutinized.

Indeed, this is so. From Bartók's letters, his statements and articles, the pictures referring to him, reminiscences of members of his family and fellow musicians we can learn much about these character-forming circumstances. We learn that Bartók's emerging personality was subject to a number of different effects and was inured by more than one crisis. As a small child he had his share of suffering. Following a smallpox inoculation in infancy he got skin disease; up to his fifth year his body was covered by a rash for which reason he did not show himself to strangers. This may be the explanation why there is no photo of him as a baby: his parents took him to the photographer only after his recovery. From this picture a serious, precocious little boy looks out at us: somebody who, in the first five years of his life, struggled with physical suffering, but also got to know the pain of companionlessness and of shame. "Poor child," his mother recollected, "he hid from people because he was hurt when they said:

'Poor little Béla!' " And hardly had he recovered, hardly had he obtained through his mother the first piano lessons—he practically wrung them from her—then a new problem arose. The family doctor declared—though perhaps on the basis of superficial observation—that the small boy had scoliosis, and he forbade him to sit. He was allowed to eat only while standing, and when he got tired he had to lie down on a rug spread on the floor and give up playing with his toys too. We can hardly be mistaken if we suppose that his psychic loneliness—which accompanied him virtually all his life—was rooted in these long and painful early illnesses.

But the sequence of these childhood afflictions was not terminated by the end of the diseases. The little boy was seven and a half years old when he lost his father. The elder Béla Bartók, headmaster of the Nagyszentmiklós Agricultural School, was a man of versatile talents: a specialist and writer on agriculture of considerable foresight, and at the same time a prolific writer of colourful travelogues. He organized a music league and an orchestra at Nagyszent-miklós and learned to play the 'cello so as to be able to participate in the ensemble. He could also play the piano and tried his hand at composing dance pieces. The fever of a short, active and full life must have practically consumed him. He died aged thirty-three...

After the father's death the bereaved family—the widow, the little boy and his sister Elza who was four years his junior—soon had to leave the headmaster's premises at the school. The mother was appointed schoolmistress first at Nagyszőllős (now Vinogradov, Carpatho-Ukraine, USSR), then at Beszterce and Pozsony (now Bistriţa, Rumania, and Bratislava, Czechoslovakia); from that time on she and her sister Irma had to worry about bringing up the two children and having them schooled. It was in these hard years full of struggle that the peerless intimacy developed between mother and son, an emotional bond that lasted through-out almost the whole of their lives, for Bartók survived by only six years his mother who died at a venerable age. And although there is no doubt that his talent for music was inherited from his father's side, it is also sure that he inherited his inclination for order and systematization from his mother, and moreover, that the way his mother reared him developed in him a striving for exactitude and truth.

Between 1899 and 1903 Bartók was a pupil in the faculties of piano and composition at the Academy of Music in Budapest. From the very beginning his masters recognized his extra-ordinary abilities; yet his years at the Academy were not ones of undisturbed progress. As early as the opening months of the first school-year he fell ill. From Pozsony his mother came post-haste to Budapest to have her son examined by a professor who stated that Bartók had bronchitis and advised him to give up music as a profession. "He should be, perhaps, a ju-rist..." If the family had followed this medical advice the musical history of the twentieth century might have taken a different course. But Bartók's desperate resistance and the wise intervention of István Thomán, his piano master, persuaded the physician to revise his opinion as well as his suggestion. Soon Bartók recovered from this illness, but in the summer of the following year he came down again with pneumonia and pleurisy. The illness seemed to be more serious on that occasion and the Bartóks' family doctor said the patient's condition was hopeless. But another doctor in Pozsony saved him and sent him to a mountain resort. The cure at Meran was a success. Recovering from the grave illness which had lasted seven and a half months, Bartók could return to Budapest, to the Academy of Music in April 1901.

As a student of piano he was always regarded there as belonging among those of outstanding talent. In his piano master István Thomán, a former pupil of Liszt, Bartók found not only a teacher of excellent attainments but also—as shown by his above-mentioned intervention—a man who carefully prepared his future course. His fellow-students respected his knowledge, but his taciturn, self-contained and sombre personality did not particularly attract them. Apart from one or two exceptions, Bartók did not seek their company either. Only the letters sent to Pozsony bear witness to the fact that, though he spoke little, he saw and heard the more.

With the unprejudiced eyes of a young man, who had made his way to Budapest from quite modest circumstances in the provinces, he observed the features at once attractive and repulsive of the capital. He recorded in his weekly reports to his mother observations, often hitting the nail on the head, on works and artists, on important and nondescript people, and on many phenomena of musical and social life.

But soon he came to a standstill in his composing. By and by he rid himself of the tone of his early pieces which bore the marks of Mendelssohn's, Schumann's and Brahms's influence. But it took him a long time to find his own voice and the new course he had been longing for. His master Hans Koessler, who taught composition in the spirit of Brahms, was hardly able to be of assistance in this respect. Bartók had reached a crisis and composed practically nothing for about two years.

The first performance in Budapest of Richard Strauss's symphonic poem *Thus Spake Zoroaster* wrenched him from this apathy in 1902. Suddenly he had a vision of a course on which it was worth while to set out: he started composing again. Almost at the same time he discovered the goal he wanted to reach by this new path. Under the influence of public opinion demanding an independent Hungary he realized his patriotic vocation: to create a distinctively Hungarian music. It was a remote goal indeed; but in a synthesis of Straussian innovation and Hungarian musical traditions he thought to have hit on the means by which to attain it.

He did not yet know folk-song—the principal source of inspiration of his later creative periods —but he knew another kind of Hungarian musical tradition: the *verbunkos*, the instrumental dance music that flourished in the nineteenth century, and its descendants, the popular-national songs composed in the spirit of the *csárdás*. The romantic Hungarian composers—Liszt, Erkel and Mosonyi—had also drawn from this well of tradition: it was the *csárdás* and the songs mentioned before that the young Bartók had heard in the small provincial towns as well as in the Budapest of the turn of the century. No wonder, that at the beginning of his career he deemed *this* tradition to be truly folk music and that he formulated the themes of his works written between 1902 and 1905 in accordance with its spirit. He elaborated these themes according to similar basic principles as those later inspired by genuine folk-songs. Thus, in 1903, the symphonic poem *Kossuth* was born and so was a *Sonata* for violin and piano, followed a year later by the *Piano Quintet* and the *Rhapsody* for piano, and for piano and orchestra, respectively. In 1905 the *Suite No. 1* and the first three movements of the *Suite No. 2* for orchestra were composed. The 1904 première of *Kossuth* in Budapest turned the young composer overnight into an artist of nationwide fame. At the time he was composing this work Bartók put his first *ars poetica* into the following words in a letter he wrote to his mother: "Everyone, on reaching maturity, has to set himself a goal, and must direct all his work and actions towards this. For my own part, all my life, in every sphere, always and in every way, I shall have one objective: the good of Hungary and of the Hungarian nation."

The success of *Kossuth*, however, proved to have been a purely local one. When, a month after the Budapest première, Hans Richter performed Bartók's work in Manchester, the work was given a mixed reception. Nor was *Kossuth* again performed during the composer's lifetime. Bartók had to realize that the recognition of foreign audiences could only be won by fighting every step of the way. It was with such considerations in mind that he went to Paris as a pianist and composer to take part in the Rubinstein music competition there. However, instead of meeting with triumph, he had to endure failure: in the piano competition Wilhelm Backhaus won the palm, whereas in the composers' competition the prize was not awarded at all. Due to the effect of the Paris failure, Bartók gave up the career of a virtuoso of the piano. Up to the end of his life he continued to give concerts, for he could not afford to abstain—and without his contribution the history of musical performing arts in the twentieth century would be incomplete—but his pianistic role was put increasingly at the service of his activity as composer in every meaning of the term.

In other respects, too, the year 1905 was a turning point in Bartók's career. With *Suite No. 1* for orchestra and the first three movements of *Suite No. 2* he appeared to have exhausted Hungarian romantic tradition as a source of inspiration. And yet all that had been inspired by *verbunkos* music, from the symphonic poem *Kossuth* up to *Suite No. 2*, was important and noteworthy. Not only was it so from a music historian's viewpoint—that is to say, because Bartók had got further than any of his Hungarian predecessors in realizing the programme of national romanticism of independent Hungarian musical composition—but also because in this romantic period of his creative work Bartók had tried out the basic principles of structure and form to be included in numerous later compositions of his. It has already been mentioned that he elaborated *verbunkos* themes—both themes taken from other composers and his own musical ideas in the spirit of the *verbunkos*—according to the same principles as he later had in mind when arranging folk-songs. But a great many other characteristics of his later creations had also already appeared in Bartók's compositions of 1902 to 1905: the sonata form inherited from Franz Liszt which extended through the whole of a work several movements long, as well as mono-thematics that forged a cycle of works into an even closer-knit unit. In the construction of a movement or of a complete work we have already encountered the symmetrical structure built around a central movement or section of a movement, that is to say, the "bridge-structure". It is here that we meet with the first examples in Bartók's œuvre of the reversal of the theme, the "sliding" of the theme, of the "exposure" of the theme's origin. Here are the first attempts at whole-tone scale, of the asymmetric rhythm models anticipating the "Bulgarian rhythms", of shorter or longer elaborations in the form of fugues or concerto grossos. And it is in these youthful works that there first appear two important types of movement characteristic of Bartók's subsequent creative period: the scherzo which is attacking, swaggering, or grotesque, and also the funeral march.

Here, as so often later on, the principle of gradualness in Bartók's development can be noticed: the peculiarities of later creative periods are rooted in earlier ones. However great the number of new, unexpected and startling turns that may appear—not only in the "next period", but already in the "next work" too—the evolution is more organic than it at first appears. Bartók takes possession of new spiritual territory by preserving, in one form or another, that already occupied. He preserves it even if, proceeding towards new shores, he seeks to rid himself of the very memory of the old.

Such a gesture of "longing to jettison" terminates Bartók's romantic-national creative period. What could be learned from the past he did learn. What new means could be tried out with regard to traditional substance he did try. Almost at the very moment when he felt that he was unable to obtain any new inspiration from those Hungarian traditions he had come to know, he began to be acquainted with folk-song, and this gave a new direction to his work. He still considered popular-national songs to be folk-songs—when, in 1904, due rather to good luck than to conscious recognition, he wrote down for the first time a genuine folk tune after hearing the singing of a Transylvanian Székely servant girl. In the following years he began systematically to collect folk-songs in the villages among the peasantry of the various regions of Hungary. It was his good luck, at the very beginning in the autumn of 1905, that he became more closely acquainted with Zoltán Kodály. Kodály's wide concept of culture, his scholarly erudition equalling his knowledge of music, his sober industriousness—which through ever-present self-control caused new results and new discoveries slowly to mature into compositions—had a signal effect on the further development of Bartók's personality. The collecting of folk-songs and the epoch-making conclusions as to composition deduced from them drew the two young men closer to each other. In the fire of common work and common plans acquaintanceship was forged into lifetime friendship.

We are indebted to Kodály's pen for one of the most appropriate features of Bartók's portrait: "*novarum rerum cupidus*" (the lover of new things). With the words of Endre Ady, the greatest

Hungarian poet of our century, Bartók could also have said of himself: "I will not be the minstrel of the grey ones." Both as a scholar and an artist he was attracted by what had never before been voiced, by the unknown. This quality—and the appeal of the *Zeitgeist*—had led him to folk-song. But he would hardly have become a scholarly explorer of folk music had he not possessed persistence and a love of work, an adoring attitude towards nature and a passion for collecting. He loved nature and everything natural in all its manifestations. He was a passionate hiker, he understood astronomy, he collected plants, minerals and also peasant embroidery and pottery; he systematized all the things he collected on the basis of what he read of their several literatures which he had studied thoroughly. According to one of his statements, he deemed folk-song also to be one of nature's manifestations. In this, too, his approach differed from Kodály's: Kodály regarded folk-song from the angle of a literary man, of a linguist and historian and not of a natural scientist. Folklore afforded different modes of inspiration to the two composers as well. When all is said and done, Bartók "learned" from folk-song about structures that might be said to have scientific foundations (mastering many an other thing in addition to these); Kodály also drew upon folk-song in order to depict poetically historical frescoes, and to see in the thousand small images that the "collective memory" of the people has preserved fragments of an epic poem which suggest the outlines of a monumental form. On the other hand, common to both was the human experience with which they became enriched in the course of their collecting tours, in addition to their acquaintance with folk-song. "At first we were trying to find only the lost tunes of the people," Kodály wrote. "But seeing rural people, their fresh vitality and the abundance of talent become lost through neglect, the picture of a cultured Hungary reborn from the people rose before our eyes. We staked our lives on its realization."

"They staked their lives"—but it was from the very experience of their travels in rural parts that they drew the creative energy for the lifetime needed. The Bartók who was known to be so reticent by his closest adherents, a man who for so long manifested himself only in his works and spoke only with his eyes, could recall with moving warmth the musical experiences as well as those others of his folk-music collecting tours: "... I may say that our wearisome work performed in this field gave greater pleasure than anything else. The days spent in villages among the peasants were the happiest in my life." Agatha Fassett's book on Bartók's years in America, in somewhat contrived terms though yet always with innate genuine respect, reveals that in those later alien surroundings the composer again and again drew strength from his old rural memories.

Of course, folk-song was only one—though one of the most important—of the influences suddenly overwhelming him. It is a peculiar mark of the genius that he can "profit" in his work from all kinds of experiences, even from such as would quite overwhelm an ordinary person. Thus not even the day of failure in Paris proved to be useless: to the young man, who had grown up in the small Hungarian provincial town and matured as man and artist on the border of the cultured Europe of those times, there suddenly unfolded the feverishly seething life of the "intellectual centre" of the world, a life of widening horizons and inspiring new possibilities. It was at about the same time that he became disillusioned with Richard Strauss and with romantic Hungarian traditions. One or two years later he got to know Debussy's new and liberating music, and from that time onward he professed the dual source of his art to be the ancient Hungarian folk music and the new French music.

For a long period after that he could not expect Hungarian audiences to be able to follow him on his course. Hungarian folk music, the music of the villages, which had preserved ancient traditions, when not unknown, was foreign to urban audiences. Remembering that, at the outset of his career, Bartók himself had not known genuine folklore, we can appreciate that for these audiences Bartók's works became more and more alien and incomprehensible when the composer extended his explorations of folk music—and thus widened the field of inspiration of his creative art—to cover Slovak folklore (1906) and Rumanian (1909). Then there were further innovations: the modal and pentatonic scales he discovered under the joint impact of folk-songs and of Debussy and the new thinking in harmonics, polytonality, chromatics that had nearly reached dodecaphony, and the application of speech-like, free and fluid rhythms. The farther Bartók was getting "from old shores" the louder grew the voices about his "having gone astray as a composer". This ever-deepening abyss between him and the audiences, and other turns that his life took—of which his letters to the talented and beautiful Hungarian violinist Stefi Geyer and the compositions connected with her reveal so much—drove Bartók into a spiritual crisis, perhaps the gravest of his youthful period. Composing helped him to overcome the crisis—and on this occasion the crisis brought masterpieces to fruition. Well might Kodály say of the *String Quartet No. 1*, composed in 1908 and completed in 1909, that this work was "a return to life". In other respects the highly significant experiments published under the title of *Bagatelles*, *Easy Piano Pieces*, *Sketches* and *Elegies*, had also been promotive to the birth of this masterpiece, these works which were partially completed becoming cycles only after the completion of the string quartet. It was through these compositions that Aladár Tóth—the most eminent Hungarian music critic of Bartók's and Kodály's era—was first able to observe the similarity of function of certain genres in Beethoven's and Bartók's œuvre: with both of them compositions for the piano were touchstones of new thoughts, whereas the string quartets were with both the most mature and most consistent terminations of certain periods.

We are indebted to Antal Molnár's observations for this meaningful sketch of the first string quartet's composer. "When ... I was commissioned by Kodály to collect folk-songs in Transylvania Bartók often received me at his flat on Teréz Boulevard... As I was inexperienced in the technique of collecting he had to provide me with instructions. He spoke as objectively as if a locksmith were introducing a new apprentice to his tools. But he did so only with half-words, with a brevity that was an honour. Otherwise he stared at me, with wide-open inquisitive eyes, in complete silence often for as long as a quarter of an hour. And as I dared not break the silence it happened that we looked at each other without uttering a word for a long time. Once he suddenly set down at the piano and played his first string quartet. When he had finished it we did not say a word for about half an hour again. We were talking silently, and, I felt, eloquently! It was only from the 1920s on that Bartók became more informal and talkative; then he could adjust better to the usual forms of everyday intercourse."

In 1909, the year he finished the first string quartet, Bartók married his pupil Márta Ziegler. In 1910 their son Béla was born. In the following year the small family moved to Rákoskeresztúr, a quiet suburb of Budapest. There two works of great importance were created in 1911. One is the *Allegro Barbaro* for piano, a composition which, with its freshness of tone, sprung from the source of folk music and which, with the constant and unflagging tension of its rhythm, is the prototype of a number of Bartók's later quicker movements. His only opera, *Bluebeard's Castle*, was also composed in the same year.

Béla Balázs's libretto gave Bartók the opportunity to integrate both modern and ancient. Balázs had drawn the elements of his theme from French legends and Transylvanian Székely folk ballad. In his ingenious style he was inspired by West-European Symbolist poetry and by the exquisite archaic wording of Székely ballads. A new psychological drama was constructed from the basic motifs of the legend and the ballad; the theme was one of the most topical and exciting of the turn of the century: the battle of the sexes, the ties and sources of conflict between man and woman. Bartók's musical solution, too, forged into regular-symmetrical symphonic structure elements both very old and very new. Numerous characteristics of ancient Hungarian folk-song—its pentatony or modality—are as typical of its melodic world as the so-called "acoustic" scale derived from overtones or the Debussy-inspired whole-tone scale. That the formation of the vocal parts, the recitative-like declamation show the joint effect of Debussy and Hungarian folk-song was observed by Bartók himself—in an indirect but unequivocal reference—in the statement he made on the death of the French composer. According to this statement Debussy's opera *Pelléas and Mélisande* "is remarkable because from the point of view of declamation it has broken with the Wagnerian method, applying instead a singular recitative-like declamation which he reached through following old French authors, a recitative distantly related with that of Hungarian parlando folk-songs." At the same time, the expressive orchestral idiom, the passionate poetry and dramatic representation in the orchestra are closer to Wagner than to Debussy, not to mention the central dramatic idea of the opera. The self-sacrificing love of the young woman which carries the only possibility of the redemption of the lonely man bears a direct relation to the idea of the *Flying Dutchman* or *Lohengrin*. For seven years *Allegro Barbaro* remained unpublished; *Bluebeard's Castle* failed at the competition for operas of the Lipótvárosi Kaszinó of Budapest. More and more undisguised was the appalling gap separating Bartók and Kodály from the public at large or the institutions of musical life. "In 1911," Bartók wrote in his autobiography, "a number of young musicians, Kodály and myself among them, tried hard to found a New Hungarian Musical Union [known by its Hungarian abbreviation UMZE]. The chief aim of the new organization would have been to form an orchestra able to perform old, new and recent music in a proper way. But we strove in vain, we could not achieve our aim. Other more personal disappointments were added to this broken plan and in 1912 I retired completely from public life. With more enthusiasm than ever I devoted myself to studies in musical folklore." It had not occurred to anybody—even Kodály realized it only later—that the transformation of public taste is a slow process, and one which need not necessarily start in the concert hall.

Bartók's letter written to the composer Géza Vilmos Zágon in August 1913 gives a faithful reflection of his state of mind at that time: "... a year ago sentence of death was officially pronounced on me as a composer. Either those people are right, in which case I am an untalented bungler; or I am right, and it's they who are the idiots... Therefore I have resigned myself to write for my writing-desk only. — So far as appearances abroad are concerned, all my efforts during the last 8 years have proved to be in vain. I got tired of it, and a year ago I stopped pressing for that, too... My public appearances are confined to *one sole field*: I will do anything to further my research work in musical folklore! I have to be personally active in this field, for nothing can be achieved in any other way; while neither recognition nor public appearances are required for composing." In 1912 he composed a single work only: the *Four Orchestral Pieces*, for his writing-desk certainly. He orchestrated them only in 1921, for up to then the possibility of their worthy rendering seemed to him to be utterly remote. His job as professor of piano at the Budapest Academy of Music, to which he had been appointed in 1907, remained practically the only link connecting him with "public appearances".

For the failures suffered in the musical life of the city he was compensated by his study of the musical life of the countryside. Affinities and divergences caused him to search out increasingly distant connections, to extend his examination over ever larger territories. In 1912 he was taken up with plans for a collecting tour of Chuwash-Tartar music in Asian Russia. As we know from Kodály's account this tour was not to be realized on account of growing military tensions. But in 1913 he succeeded in getting as far as North Africa, where he studied the folk music of the Arabs in the vicinity of Biskra. The discoveries of the scholar did not fail to produce, on this occasion also, an effect on the composer; years, even decades, later strains of Arab folk music emerged in some portions of the *Suite* for piano, in *String Quartet No. 2*, *The Miraculous Mandarin* and the *Dance Suite*, as well as in some pieces of the *Duos* and the *Mikrokosmos*.

The breaking out of the First World War blighted the realization of his large-scale programme of folk-song research. For a considerable time Bartók himself was unable to do any work: "The events upset me to such an extent that they almost paralysed me," he wrote to Ion Bianu, librarian of the Rumanian Academy of Sciences on September 17, 1914. In these hard weeks and months he was kept going by the hope that he would be able to continue his scientific work even though under changed circumstances: "What I would wish most of all is that peace should be maintained at least between ourselves and Rumania. But whatever may occur, I will remain faithful to the work I have begun: I consider it the purpose of my life to continue and complete the investigation of Rumanian folk music, at least in Transylvania."

Fortunately, Bartók did not have to do military service. "I've been rejected as unfit for service (lack of stamina)," he informed Ion Buşiţia, his Rumanian friend in Transylvania, in May 1915. He added "...they're quite right, too, with only 45 kg to help me along I would find it a bit of an effort to do big marches or quick advances (or retreats?) and with a great load on my back, too."

In the same letter he mentioned "the state of depression," which "in my case, alternates with a kind of devil-may-care attitude". But he also wrote that he had succeeded in continuing his work of collecting Slovakian folk-songs first in his own locality (Rákoskeresztúr), and then in Zólyom County in the north. The fact that Rumania entered the war in 1916 was a heavy blow to him. For years he had feared this possibility; he was afraid—and his fears were well justified—that this step would deprive him of the conditions under which he could continue collecting Rumanian folk music. Of this period "...the last 18 months have brought me more troubles than I've had during the rest of my life." This from Bartók, who so rarely complained and carefully weighed the significance of his words, writing to Buşiţia in May 1917. "The steadily worsening world situation which, it seems, has ruined my career (collecting folk-songs, I mean), for the most beautiful regions of all, Eastern Europe and the Balkans, are completely ravaged—this in itself has depressed me enough." In 1918 his collecting tours with a phonograph came to an end; after a break of almost two decades he ventured only once more, in 1936, to set out on a folk-song collecting expedition in the region of Adana along the Syrian border in Turkey. Instead of being devoted to collecting new material, decades in the life of Bartók the folk-music scholar were to be occupied with revising, systematizing and comparing the old materials several times, and by summarizing the results he had allowed to mature.

For a time the outbreak of war depressed the creative buoyancy of Bartók which had seemed to have come to new life. He set aside the newly-begun stage work, the composition of the ballet *The Wooden Prince*, again to Béla Balázs's libretto; on account of "paralysing anxiety" and "depression caused by the war", not a single work left his studio in 1914. But in the next year he wrote a whole group of new pieces. As if surprised himself, he informed Buşiţia: "I have even found the time—and ability—to do some composing." He drew new strength from folk music, this time from Rumanian folk music. In Bartók's life 1915 was the year of the "Rumanian compositions" and, at the same time, of interesting experiments in forms of "pure" folk-song material (that is to say, such as does not need horizontal completion by the composer).

Sonatina, condensing the themes of Rumanian folk-songs into a classic framework, was followed by the cycle of *Rumanian Folk Dances*, dedicated to Buşiţia and then by the two series of *Rumanian Christmas Carols (Colindas);* then there came two vocal compositions, unpublished up to this very day: *Two Rumanian Folk-Songs* for female chorus and *Nine Rumanian Songs* for voice and piano.

Ever since the *Two Rumanian Dances* and the *Allegro Barbaro* it could be observed that the rhythmic skeleton of the compositions had grown firmer; and since *Bluebeard's Castle* and the *Four Orchestral Pieces*, a greater concentration of form and content had emerged. These are important characteristics of the creative period which began with the "Rumanian compositions". "In his youthful works the surge of life was seeking outlet in voluble and agitated forms, multicoloured but somewhat loose in their structure"—thus Kodály, referring to the compositions preceding *String Quartet No. 1*. "Later on ever-increasing concentration drove out of

16

them everything superfluous that did not belong to their essence." Such a creation, laconic and yet conveying so much, is the *Suite* for piano composed in 1916. It is in a strange, rather oblique manner that folklore influenced it. In all probability it was while studying the instrumental folk music of East-European peoples that Bartók became aware of the folk-dance roots of baroque concertos. Behind the initial movement of the *Suite* can be felt the throb of rapid concerto grosso movements as also that of certain types of folk-dance tunes. And all this years before the appearance of musical neo-classicism! The force of the earlier savage scherzo and allegro barbaro movements is enhanced in the faster pieces in the *Suite*; in these the type of "rushing" movements came into being which were to play so important a role in Bartók's later work, from *The Miraculous Mandarin* up to the piano pieces written in the late twenties, the *String Quartets Nos. 3* and *4* and the *Cantata Profana*. After the "reckless", the "demoniac", the "barbaric" and "formidably strong" movements Bartók concludes the *Suite* with a slow movement. Thus he gives the last word to the thrilling poetry of loneliness which, although not of this degree of concentration in form and content, had appeared earlier in the *Laments*, in the *Bluebeard's Castle* opera's scene of the "lake of tears" and in the funeral march of the *Four Orchestral Pieces*. It is in the same shattering manner—with a slow finale—that he wound up the two cycles of songs composed in 1915–1916 and the *String Quartet No. 2* written between 1915 and 1917. The "folk-dance finale" he had brought into being after experimenting with it in the Rumanian piano pieces, in the *Fifteen Hungarian Peasant Songs*, and in the *Four Slovak Folk-Songs* that is more or less contemporaneous with the piano pieces, proved to be a more final solution for terminating composition. With few exceptions it appears in almost every one of Bartók's subsequent cyclic compositions, from the *Sonatas No. 1* and *No. 2* for violin and piano (1921–1922) up to the *Concerto No. 3* for piano and orchestra (1945).

The ballet *The Wooden Prince*, whose completion was also achieved by the year 1916, is a summary of his earlier stylistic endeavours. Nature magic—once again, though, now for the last time inspired by Wagner—a scene constructed of folk-song-like models, an unfolding of the earlier grotesque scherzo tone, the poetry of passion, gesture and motion filling the framework of a great scene—all find a place as characteristic components in the symphonic structure of the ballet.

But *The Wooden Prince* marked a stage of signal importance in Bartók's career also, because its Budapest world première on the 12th of May 1917 brought for the composer his first significant success with the audience—since the national-romantic creations of his youth—and terminated his five years' "internal exile". "The year 1917," Bartók wrote in his autobiography, "brought a change in the attitude of the Budapest public towards my compositions. I had the wonderful luck to hear a major work of mine, a musical play with the title *The Wooden Prince*, performed in a perfect manner under the direction of Maestro Egisto Tango. It was Tango who in 1918 also arranged the performance of an older one-act play, *Bluebeard's Castle*."

After the First World War and the downfall of the Austro–Hungarian Monarchy Bartók, along with Dohnányi and Kodály, was a member of the Musical Directory headed by Béla Reinitz during the Hungarian Republic of Councils. A host of reforms in musical life was expected to be carried out by the Republic of Councils: the foundation of a museum of folk music, and the introduction of new and more up-to-date methods of music teaching. However, no time remained and no chance was given for their realization. After the fall of the Republic of Councils in 1919 Reinitz was imprisoned, Dohnányi and Kodály were sent on compulsory leave, and disciplinary action was instituted against the latter. Seeing "how pretty bleak the outlook is at home" the idea of emigration came to Bartók for the first time in his life: "...I have been making what enquiries I can in 3 different countries about the chances of making a living," he wrote to his mother and aunt on October 23, 1919. "For in this country, though one can make a living, for the next 10 years at least it will not be possible to do any work, i.e. the kind of work I am interested in (studying folk music). In other words, if I have a chance to do this kind of work abroad, I see no point in staying here; and if it's impossible to make a living from this kind of work abroad either, it would still be better to teach music, in Vienna, say, than in Budapest; for there at least they have good musical institutions (orchestras, opera, etc.), whereas everything is being ruined here because our best musicians, our only ones—Tango, Dohnányi, etc.—are being hounded out of their posts." Indeed, in February 1920 he went to Berlin to gather information, and it was there that he gave his first concerts abroad after the war. He spent nearly three months in the German capital—only to return to Hungary again. "...As you know well, the folk-songs would hardly let me go westwards; all in vain: they are drawing me to the east," he wrote at the end of March to Busiţia from Berlin.

On his return he put an end to his residence in the suburb, which had lasted nearly a decade, and with his family moved into the hospitable home of the banker József Lukács, father of Georg Lukács, the philosopher. The two years he spent there, amidst very difficult external circumstances, provided him with the possibility of undisturbed work. And it was in this house, in the company of the Lukács family, that he met Thomas Mann, the greatest figure in contemporary German literature.

How "pretty bleak the outlook" was in the Hungary of the 1920s is shown by the assault launched in the press against Bartók. When a scholarly work of his on Rumanian folk music in Transylvania that had been previously published in Hungarian many years before came out in German, the music correspondent of the *Nemzeti Újság* flared up in protest, seemingly having discovered in it anti-Hungarian political tendencies and even "unpatriotic poison". Jenő Hubay, the new director of the Academy of Music, chimed in, essentially repeating the accusations against Bartók. In an article couched in strong language Bartók answered his attackers. And "in the name of freedom to undertake scientific research," his cause was supported by the board of the Hungarian Ethnological Society. Such similar attacks, whether political or would-be scholarly, were instigated now by Hungarian and now by Rumanian nationalists, and were to accompany time and time again Bartók's career as folk-music researcher.

The growing appreciation abroad compensated for the difficulties and assaults he had to put up with at home. In 1918 he signed an agreement with Vienna Universal Edition regarding his compositions still in manuscript and those he intended to write. "This is a great thing," he wrote to Busiţia, "because, for about six years, nothing by me has been published thanks to Hungarian publishers... Anyhow, this contract is the greatest success I have scored as a composer up to now." Bartók's connection with Universal Edition lasted until the annexation of Austria to the German Reich. Afterwards the London firm of Boosey & Hawkes published his new works. Indeed the 1918 contract meant a decisive step towards the more widespread performance of Bartók's music: from that time on both older and newer compositions gained greater international publicity in the concert halls and opera houses of Europe. In 1919 one of his orchestral works, the *Two Pictures* composed in 1910, was performed in America, under the baton of Edgar Varèse at Carnegie Hall.

The decade of the 1920s was the period of Bartók's emergence to prominence in the musical life first of Europe and then of America. Antal Molnár's words quoted above: "he became more informal and talkative," and "could adjust himself better to the usual forms of everyday intercourse," refer to the fact that the increasing appreciation slowly melted away the thick ice of Bartók's reticence. Outstanding performing artists took his part. In addition to the conductors already mentioned, Ernst von Dohnányi, Eugen Szenkár, Fritz Reiner, Willem Mengelberg, Wilhelm Furtwängler, Václav Talich, Sir Henry Wood, Serge Koussevitzky, Erich Kleiber, Pierre Monteux, István Strasser, Josef Krips, Hermann Scherchen, Hermann Abendroth—and on some special occasions Bruno Walter and Clemens Krauss. Eminent instrumentalists interpreted his works: Jelly d'Arányi, Stefi Geyer, Joseph Szigeti, Zoltán Székely, Imre Waldbauer, Jenő Kerpely, André Gertler, Otto Herz and such outstanding celebrities among Hungarian singers as Mária Basilides, Ilona Durigo, Vilma Medgyaszay, and Ferenc Székelyhidy. But this significant list is far from complete; from the thirties on it came to be enriched with further names: Pablo Casals, Otto Klemperer, Eugene Ormandy, Antal Doráti, Louis Kentner, Ede Zathureczky, Sir Adrian Boult, Ernest Ansermet, Carl Schuricht, Sergio Failoni, Tibor Serly, Eduard van Beinum, Paul Sacher, Ferenc Fricsay, János Ferencsik and Benny Goodman put their art at the service of propagating Bartók's works. We may add the names of artists who joined the ranks of Bartók interpreters in the last years of the composer's life: Dimitri Mitropoulos, Tossy Spyvakovsky, Yehudi Menuhin, Gyorgy Sándor, and William Primrose—the first performances of the *Sonata for Solo Violin, Concerto No. 3* for piano and orchestra and *Concerto* for viola and orchestra being linked with the latter three. Moreover, some chamber-music ensembles already in the composer's lifetime espoused his art: the Waldbauer–Kerpely, the Kolisch, the Roth and the Pro Arte String Quartets—not forgetting the most authentic performer of the piano pieces, the composer himself (who was joined after 1938 in concerts for two pianos by a worthy pupil and faithful follower, his second wife, Ditta Pásztory, whom he married in 1923). Thus we have outlined, though only in a very sketchy way, the ever-widening circle of the propagators of Bartók's music.

As early as 1917 the progressive Hungarian journal of literature and art entitled MA (Today) honoured the composer of *The Wooden Prince* with a special Bartók number; a similar commemorative publication, the Bartók issue of the Vienna *Musikblätter des Anbruch*, appeared in 1921 on the occasion of the composer's fortieth birthday. Also in 1921 came out the first scholarly analysis of his music: Antal Molnár, who had previously devoted a brilliant paper to *Bluebeard's Castle*, now wrote a pioneering study on the *Two Elegies*.

In the early decades of his creative life, side by side with the discovery of folk-song, the art of Strauss and Debussy also exerted a fruitful influence on Bartók's imagination. But along with these direct musical influences, mention must be made of the effect personal acquaintance with Ferruccio Busoni and Frederic Delius had on him, giving encouragement and stimulation, and broadening his horizons. Then, in the late 1910s and at the beginning of the twenties, the influence of Schoenberg and Stravinsky made itself felt on the Hungarian composer. It was the works of Schoenberg that he encountered first. In 1909 together with Kodály he studied the Viennese master's *First String Quartet*. Soon after he secured the score of Schoenberg's *Three Pieces for Piano* op. 11, first in manuscript and later in the form of printed sheet music. They never became close or intimate, but from about 1910 they followed each other's career with mutual interest. In the *Harmonielehre* that Schoenberg completed in 1911 he twice referred to Bartók and quoted an example from his 10th Bagatelle. Denijs Dille published the two letters that Schoenberg wrote to Bartók before and after the First World War, respectively. Dille's research also revealed that in 1916 Bartók had taken part in the successful intervention aimed at having Schoenberg exempted from military service. It is a feature of the history of their connection that at the private concerts organized by Schoenberg of the Vienna Verein für Musikalische Privataufführungen, seven works by Bartók were performed between November 1918 and October 1920, that is to say in less than two years. Among these were the *Four Dirges*, the *Fourteen Bagatelles*, the *String Quartet No. 1*, the *Two Rumanian Dances* and the series of *Rumanian Folk Dances*. Of no less importance were Bartók's two publications dating from 1920 and 1921: "Das Problem der neuen Musik" (published by *Melos* in Berlin) and "Arnold Schönbergs Musik in Ungarn" (in the Vienna *Musikblätter des Anbruch*). The latter is notable because it is a demonstrative manifestation of sympathy; apart from Schoenberg among his contemporaries only to Strauss, Delius, Debussy, Kodály, and Ravel did Bartók devote whole articles or statements. The Berlin article is of theoretical significance. It treats atonality as a logical stage in the development of the history of music and as it were, provides a "theoretical background" for the *Studies*, the *Improvisations* and the two *Sonatas* for violin and piano, those of Bartók's works which were closest to the Viennese

School. "The music of our day is definitely moving towards atonality," Bartók declares. On the "equal treatment of the twelve semitones equal with one another" he states that "this new approach has immeasurable new possibilities in store". However, the article does not leave any room for doubt but that Bartók, though aware of all this, also wishes in the future to retain his "freedom of action" in composing. "Nevertheless, it does not seem correct," he writes in the same article "if we consider the principle of tonality as an absolute opposite of the principle of atonality. The latter is much more the consequence of evolution slowly unfolding from tonality, a development that proceeds with inexorable gradualness and without any interruption or violent deviation." Next: "For it is not ... the question of two diametrically opposed principles; — as I see it, well-judged (not too frequent) use of the chording of the old tonal phraseology does not clash with the style of atonal music." Thus, about 1920, "tonal" and "atonal" principles were reconciled in Bartók's theory and practice. He considered "horizontally" (melodically) and "vertically" (harmonically) the principles of "the equal treatment of twelve semitones equal with one another", as acceptable as realizing the principles of horizontal and vertical structure inspired by "folk-song models". These theoretical principles and the inferences drawn from them in the form of compositions reveal that in fact the courses of Bartók and Schoenberg did but cross and never ran parallel. Each sought—and found—what he deemed right in his own way. That is why those comparisons in which one is measured with the yardstick of the other, and which try to demonstrate what one master realized from the aims of the other (and the other way round), are unjust. Some years after having composed the *Sonatas* for violin and piano, looking back from a certain remove at developments around 1920, Bartók renounced the idea of pursuing the "Schoenbergian course" with more or less the same argument as the one he put forth in 1920, in renouncing the idea of emigration. "It is true," he wrote in 1928, "that at that time I was drawing close to a kind of dodecaphonic composition. But it is an unmistakable characteristic of my works of that period that they are built upon a tonal base." And in another passage: "No doubt, the fact that some twentieth-century composers went back to folk-song is a point of no less importance in that it impeded the atonal trend's gaining ground." Nevertheless dodecaphonic theme models did appear at time in Bartók's later works, for example in the first movement of the great *Violin Concerto*.

Bartók also knew the two other masters of the new Viennese School, although he had no close connections with either. He met Alban Berg at the international festivals of modern music in Salzburg and Florence, but it is not possible to detect evidence of any personal contact between them on the basis of those of Bartók's letters known so far or in Berg's detailed reports on his travels. It is a fact, however, that their appreciation of each other was mutual. Berg's *Lyric Suite* made a great impact on Bartók and there is proof that the latter, before writing his own *Violin Concerto* (1937–38) studied Berg's *Violin Concerto*. In the course of her talks with the present writer, Frau Helene Berg, Berg's widow, spoke about the respect the Viennese composer felt towards Bartók. The connection between Bartók and Webern was even more tenuous: at one of the concerts of the Viennese Workers' Symphonic Orchestra organized by Webern, Bartók himself played the piano part of his *Concerto No. 1* for piano on the 6th of November, 1927 (Bartók's work was conducted by István Strasser). At the same concert Kodály's *Psalmus Hungaricus* was conducted by Webern.

We have already mentioned the organic character of Bartók's development; namely, that the characteristics of his later creative periods are usually rooted in the earlier ones. This is not contradicted by the fact that Bartók, like every genuine creative artist, expressed something new with every work and surprised his contemporaries at every première with unexpected and abrupt departures. Subsequent analyses have proved that his evolution was not one of "radical innovation" in the sense of phases opposite to and contrasting with, previous stages of development. Its course was at times steep, at others less so—but it was always logical and unbroken.

Of "external influences" he absorbed whatever he needed and as much as he needed—or more exactly, for the reception of which he was internally "prepared". That these "external influences" always fertilized existing seeds of ideas may be observed when considering the circumstances of Schoenberg's inspiration and also that of Stravinsky.

Which of Stravinsky's works did Bartók know and when did he come to know them? According to an article he wrote in 1920 "we know well what Stravinsky wrote up to 1917, at least we know it from the scores". If we only consider the chief works completed until then he must have known in addition to *Fireworks* the music of the three "Russian" ballets (The *Firebird, Petrushka* and *Le Sacre du Printemps*), and also the *Rossignol, Pribaoutki* and the *Berceuses du Chat*. Bartók referred to most of these compositions in different writings of his. In the *Rossignol* he recognized Schoenberg's influence; in *Pribaoutki* he was puzzled by the joint effect of folk themes of a tonal character and by the instrumental accompaniment "consisting of a series of more or less atonal areas of tones". Mme. Márta Ziegler, Bartók's first wife, told the present writer that at the beginning of 1919 they had learned the *Sacre du Printemps* from a piano score for four hands. In this way they wanted to bring it to the attention of Dohnányi, the newly elected president-conductor of the Budapest Philharmonic Society. Mme. Bartók practised her part for several weeks, but at the "house première" Dohnányi sat at the piano with Bartók; although it was only to an intimate circle, the "Sacre" was thus first performed in Hungary by them. This story also proves how keenly Bartók was interested, already at the time when he was composing *The Miraculous Mandarin*, in Stravinsky's great *"Allegro Barbaro"*. In his writings he discussed the *Sacre* several times, calling it (along with the cantata *Les Noces*) the apotheosis of Russian folk music. He paid particular attention to its novel form, with its incessant repetition of ostinato-like short motifs. Such a ceaseless repetition of primitive motifs has, as he put it, even in folk music "quite a strange, feverishly exciting and arousing effect... This effect is enhanced a hundred times if, with the most precise calculation of the weight of their relationship, such a wizard as Stravinsky makes these motifs chase one another and pile up crushingly one upon the other."

The influence of the *Sacre du Printemps* can be recognized in Bartók's ballet *The Miraculous Mandarin* and even more so in the score of his *Dance Suite;* the cantata *Les Noces* likewise influenced the cycle called *Village Scenes*, based on Slovak folk-songs. Later Bartók was interested in Stravinsky's "neo-classical" creations; however, the Russian's stylizations of jazz, such as the *Piano Rag Music*, made no impression on him whatsoever. From the late thirties onwards he included Stravinsky's 1935 *Concerto* in the programme of his concerts for two pianos. Their rare personal meetings did not leave any deep impression on either of them. Obviously, Bartók's interest did not extend beyond the Russian master's compositions to Stravinsky himself; in turn, the few rather peculiar remarks made quite a long time after Bartók's death by Stravinsky to his assistant Robert Craft, reveal a lack of deeper understanding, though not of appreciation.

The quotations enumerated above all prove that about 1920 Bartók, while firmly grounding his art on folk music—was incessantly seeking for its synthesis with the most modern means of expression in art-music. As we have seen, at one time he deemed it possible to proceed from tonal folk music and its blending with the principles of atonal development. Later on, as is proved by a lecture given in 1931, he renounced this possibility: "...folk music is exclusively tonal," he said, "atonal folk music is something quite unthinkable. Thus, atonal 'Zwölftonmusik' cannot be based on tonal folk music, this would be patent absurdity." Among his works the two *Sonatas* for violin and piano were written as experiments at such unity. There is no doubt that, of all of Bartók's works, these are closest to Schoenberg's expressionism—but in the dance-like throb of their final movements, the inspiration of folk music's theme-models makes itself felt. The uncompromising effect of these latter is characteristic of Bartók's next major composition, the *Dance Suite* for orchestra. Along with Kodály's *Psalmus Hungaricus* Bartók classified this piece in the category of compositions inspired by folklore, works which "even if they do not utilize folk-songs specifically... do reflect the spirit of peasant music even in their most minute details."

The *Dance Suite*—consisting of five dances, a ritornelle and finale which reveals the new direction of the composer's experimentation—is an important landmark in Bartók's ideological development. It was the anniversary of the unification of Pest and Buda into Budapest; its première was at the gala concert on November 19, 1923, at which Dohnányi's *Festival Overture* and Kodály's *Psalmus Hungaricus* also were first performed. It is edifying to examine how Budapest's three leading composers expressed the idea of celebration in their works. Dohnányi achieved it with a "romantic counterpoint", "unifying" in the final movement of his Overture the themes of Erkel's *National Anthem*, Egressy's *Appeal* and his own *Hungarian Creed*. Kodály gave new relevance to the words of the psalm paraphrase of Mihály Vég, a sixteenth-century Hungarian preacher, thereby scourging the "pretty bleak" outlook in Hungary so often mentioned in Bartók's letters; thus he was able as it were to deliver a rebuff to the "official celebrants". In Bartók the word "unification" inspired ideas to which he remained faithful to the day of his death: the ideas of the brotherhood of peoples and of folk music being above the individual nations. We shall better understand the intellectual background of the *Dance Suite*, in which a homogeneous musical language was formed from Hungarian, Rumanian and Arabic theme-models, if we recall one of the hypotheses of Bartók, the folk-music researcher: "...I suspect that by the time sufficient material and results of the investigations into folk music are at our disposal, we shall see that the music of all the peoples of the world can be traced back to some common basis of primeval forms, primeval types and primeval styles." Thus the same Bartók, who, in his youth was moved by his strong nationalistic feelings to discover Hungarian folk music, and whose exactness, sense of responsibility and inner compulsion to get to the bottom of everything, made him study the folk music first of the Magyars' neighbours, and then that of more and more distant peoples—reaching after two decades the principle of the power that is "above nations", of a folk music of the world uniting millions of people.

From 1926 on new features appeared in Bartók's works, which this time did not lack "internal preparation" either. Stravinsky's example and the study of Bach and even earlier composers matured Bartók's "Neo-Classical" period. Let us not forget that there had previously been instances in his works of fugue and fugato-like elaborations, reversal of theme, and throbbing baroque motifs. But in the cycles for the piano, in the chamber-music works and orchestral compositions written between 1926 and 1931 *(Sonata* for piano; *Out of Doors, Nine Little Piano Pieces, Concertos No. 1* and *No. 2, Three Rondos on Folk Tunes, String Quartets Nos. 3* and *4, Cantata Profana* and some pieces of the *Mikrokosmos)* these "neo-classical" features came to the fore along with the intensified force and surging dynamism of the "allegro barbaros". Linear polyphony and the driving rhythms of the rapid concerto grosso movements were given important roles; imitations, two-part inventions, canons, fugues and various theme-reversions also appeared. In the late twenties Bartók encountered again—in Kodály's masterpieces and in his own studies of instrumental folk music—the *verbunkos*, the music of the Hungarian community of his youth. Or to put it more exactly, he encountered the old type of *verbunkos* rooted in folk music, the type he did not know in his earlier years. And from that time onwards the *verbunkos* models again made an appearance among the means Bartók used, from the two *Rhapsodies, Contrasts*, and the first movement originally indicated as "Tempo di Verbunkos" of the great *Violin Concerto* up to the *Divertimento* and *Concerto No. 3* for piano. It is again the two *Rhapsodies*, those "peasant-baroque violin concertos" which may lead us to think that the study of East-European instrumental folk music caused Bartók to hypothesize that the baroque violin concertos had sprung from instrumental folk-dance music. All these innovations of the idiom—to which are added enrichment and differentiation of orchestration and tone colour in general—are achievements which Bartók held to and evolved to a greater or lesser degree all his life. These achievements, having finally found their place in the composer's universe, became his very own personal idiom to such an extent that after 1931 we cannot speak of any "external" influences apart from some intentional musical quotations.

From the second half of the twenties it can be observed how Bartók's slow movements, previously softly melancholic and sad, became gradually imbued with the tones and mysterious soft noises of nature and of the night, with their anguish and awful loneliness. How meaningful, how fraught with signification, how animated the "silence" of nature is for Bartók! In these great nocturnal pictures—which on the basis of one of the pieces of the 1926 cycle *Out of Doors* we term the "music of the night" type of movement—Bartók gave utterance to such things about nature and man as nobody had done before.

About 1930 these nature themes became extended in his works by means of a new group of thoughts: Bartók protested against the greedy mechanization, against a sham civilization that brought about the destruction of the old natural values: that is to say, against the alienation of man from nature. It is in this sense that he professes a "return to nature", to that "clean source", in the *Cantata Profana* (1930), his grand work for double mixed chorus, tenor and baritone solists and orchestra, whose Hungarian verses based on Rumanian *colindas* were written by Bartók himself.

This "clean source" is an expression that appears again in a letter the composer wrote in 1931 to a Rumanian follower of his, Octavian Beu: "My own idea, however—of which I have been fully conscious since I found myself as a composer—is the brotherhood of peoples, brotherhood in spite of all wars and conflicts. I try—to the best of my ability—to serve this idea in my music; therefore I don't reject any influence, be it Slovakian, Rumanian, Arabic or from any other source. The source must only be clean, fresh and healthy!" Suffice it to compare this quotation with his patriotic *ars poetica* written to his mother in 1903, to perceive the expansion of his horizon. And yet, the 1931 *ars poetica* does not "annul" the first; it rather completes its message and raises it to a higher level. What Bartók himself said to Bence Szabolcsi about his artistic evolution can be referred to his human development too: it is like a spiral, raising what has already existed to ever higher levels.

In the 1930s the gradual maturing of the slow movements appears to illustrate this statement. Bartók's taking refuge in primeval nature at its clean source may evidently partly be due to the contemporary ideological-political ferment; the signs and consequences of this break from the 1930s onwards bore more and more harshly upon the artist who, although withdrawing from the skirmishes of political life, keenly observed the transformation of his surroundings and reacted accordingly. In May 1931 the Italian fascists beat up Arturo Toscanini, the great conductor of the period, and induced him to leave Italy immediately because he refused to conduct the *Giovinezza*, the fascist march. Bartók was personally connected with Toscanini only in the sense of being a similar fanatic of truth expressed in terms of music. But he wrote in indignation to the Oxford Meeting of the International Society of Contemporary Music, on behalf of the "protection of the freedom of the art", protesting against "outrageous interference" by "factors extraneous to art" into artistic life. Apart from his letters, it is the slow movements of his works that reveal most faithfully how the intrusion, more and more intense, of these "factors extraneous to art" not only into artistic life but into the life of the whole of Europe, affected Bartók. In these slow movements the awesome voice of nature becomes increasingly permeated with a note of horror, of anguish and of premonition of approaching disaster (*Music for String Instruments, Percussion and Celesta*, 1936, *Sonata for Two Pianos and Percussion*, 1937, *Divertimento* for string orchestra, 1939). We cannot but think of the Hungarian folk-song, and of the lines of the poet Attila József citing that folk-song: "He who wants to be a piper, must go to the fire of hell. There he must learn, learn and master, how to blow his pipe quite well." It was as if the profound symbols of these lines came to be consummated in Bartók's art at that time. For, simultaneously with his descent into the hells of the emotions—seeking as it were for answers and prophecies—those final movements hymnic in nature came into being which, up to the very last, ended his works on a hopeful and elevating note. A singular contrast illumines the internal world of these works: the rigorous laws laid down by himself, of symmetry and structure—the discovery of which is to the credit of Ernő Lendvai—moreover went side by side, in a gradual simplification and purification of the expression and the message with an extreme subjectivity.

These latter great works as we have mentioned were born in the menacing shadow of world disaster approaching more and more closely. After the world première of his *Concerto No. 2* for piano and orchestra in Frankfurt a. Main, January 23, 1933, Bartók refused to give any more recitals in Germany. The so-called Anschluss, Austria's outrageous annexation to Germany, was a heavy blow to him. Of this he wrote on April 13, 1938 to his confidante adherent Mme. Annie Müller-Widmann in Basel that he feared "the imminent danger that Hungary will surrender to this regime of thieves and murderers. The only question is—when and how? And how I can then go on living in such a country or—which means the same thing—working, I simply cannot conceive. As a matter of fact, I would feel it my duty to emigrate, so long as that were possible."

In the summer of 1939 at Saanen in Switzerland as Paul Sacher's guest and at his request he composed the *Divertimento* for string orchestra and a considerable part of the *String Quartet No. 6*. At that time he did not know himself that these were the last works he was to write in Europe—indeed, they were almost the last pieces of his œuvre. By the time he returned from Switzerland he found his mother incurably ill; at the end of the year she passed away. With his mother's death the last link appeared to have broken that had connected Bartók with a Hungary on the brink of the abyss. In April 1940 he went for a month's concert tour to the United States, with a view to investigate possibilities there. He returned for a few months; on the 8th of October 1940 he played at a concert with his wife at the Academy of Music in Budapest. That was the occasion of his farewell to Hungarian, and indeed European, audiences. On the 12th of October he left Hungary and travelled across Italy, Switzerland, the South of France, Spain, and Portugal to embark at Lisbon for New York on the 20th. "This voyage is actually, like plunging into the unknown from what is known but unbearable," he wrote in his last letter to Mme. Müller-Widmann. "But we have no choice, it isn't at all the question whether this must happen; for it must happen." It was hardly chance that Bartók—as he so often did in his music—quoted Beethoven here too: the motto of the final movement entitled: *Der schwer gefasste Entschluss* of the *String Quartet* in F Major, op. 135: "*Muss es sein? Es muss sein! Es muss sein!*"

The span of nearly five years that he spent from the end of October 1940 up to his death in the United States was divided into two contrasting periods. The manner of his very arrival was an ominous omen: with the exception of his hand luggage, all of his luggage together with a significant part of his œuvre as a composer and scholar in the form of manuscripts was held up, due to the complicated customs examinations and the great rush and confusion, first at the Spanish–Portuguese border and then at Lisbon. Only in February of the next year did Bartók receive the luggage indispensable for the continuation of his work, at a time when he had long given up ever obtaining them.

His first years in America showed signs of increasing depression; arthritis appeared in his left shoulder, the first symptom of subsequent mortal disease. The number of his concerts with his wife was decreasing. In 1940, 1941 and 1942 not a single new composition was born; he only completed some transcriptions: the *Concerto for Two Pianos, Percussion and Orchestra* and the *Suite for Two Pianos* (in the former he expanded the dimension of the *Sonata for Two Pianos and Percussion*, in the latter he reduced his orchestral work, *Suite No. 2*, which he had composed between 1905 and 1907). Both the external and internal peace and quiet needed for concentrated work were missing; he was tortured by growing homesickness and by increasing anxiety at Hungary's fate. Columbia University, which conferred on him an honorary degree as early as

November 1940, secured for him a modest but permanent income by commissioning him to notate and prepare for publication the Milman Parry Serbo-Croatian collection of folk music.

In spite of all this, Bartók was unable to strike roots in America. The life and mentality of the place were basically alien to him. There too as at home he avoided publicity; apart from his concerts and publications, he fought shy of all kinds of proselytizing about his name and works. In this respect he adhered to the principle he had expounded as early as 1937 to his Belgian devotee and biographer, Denijs Dille, the publisher later on of many of his compositions and scholarly works: "I have composed music and will compose music as long as I am alive; this music then is to hold its own and speak for itself... in this it does not need my help." Leukemia, his mortal illness that was not disclosed to him by his doctors up to the very end was gradually overcoming him with varying intensity, but more and more implacably. No doubt, in the first years the "external world" failed—apart from one or two unwavering adherents of the composer's—to do what it ought to have done for Béla Bartók. "Otherwise, my career as a composer is as much as finished," he wrote on New Year's Eve 1942 to his former pupil Mrs. Wilhelmine Creel. "The quasi boycott of my works by leading orchestras continues, no performances of either old work[s] or new ones. It is a shame—not for me, of course." In his whole life which had not lacked of crises, perhaps never since the writing of the first string quartet may Bartók have felt at such a low ebb, so hopeless and so lonely.

True, it was difficult to "help" Bartók. America was overwhelmed by millions of European refugees—and official public opinion could hardly be expected to pay attention to the Hungarian musician of unobtrusive appearance who never asked anybody for anything. On the other hand, Bartók himself did not make helping him an easy business. Only a few people really knew his personality; he had only a few true adherents and friends such as Pál Kecskeméti and his wife, the harpsichord artist Erzsébet Láng, the composer-conductor Tibor Serly, his physician Doctor Holló, the pianist Erno Balogh and the folk-music researcher George Herzog. Apart from the members of his family and the small circle of friends, nobody could scale or see through the "stone wall" of obdurate reticence erected by Bartók against intruders real or supposed, who might endanger his work. Only a few people could obtain proof of the subtle and natural simplicity of his individuality, his peculiar humour, and the deep sympathy he felt for those he loved and appreciated. But even his closest adherents had soon to come to accept his unrelenting consistency in financial-ethical questions; the fact, for example, that he never accepted any "support" from anybody under any circumstances whatsoever, not even when in the gravest difficulties. He had a morbid horror of accepting money that he had not worked for.

And yet, early in 1943, when he was at the nadir both physically and intellectually, support that was acceptable to him did emerge. As a result of the work behind the scenes in his interest by his old and enthusiastic devotee Erno Balogh, the ASCAP (American Society of Composers, Authors and Publishers) undertook to pay for Bartók's medical treatment and for his summer rest period although he was not a member of the Society. In all likelihood, the composer never had any knowledge of the considerable sum devoted by ASCAP to his recovery, nor of the unflagging work in his interest of Deems Taylor, President of the Society, and his secretary Sylvia Rosenberg.

In the summer of 1943 a sudden improvement in Bartók's health was noticeable. It was about this time, upon Joseph Szigeti's advice, that the famous conductor Serge Koussevitzky visited him in convalescence and asked him, on behalf of the Nathalie Koussevitzky Foundation, to write an orchestral work. The commission put new life into Bartók and—thanks to the temporary improvement of his condition—he wrote, at the Saranac Lake resort in New York State, his *Concerto for Orchestra* within some fifty-five days. After three years' silence as a composer this work introduced his last creative period. The *Concerto for Orchestra* was followed in 1944 by the *Sonata for Solo Violin*, composed for Yehudi Menuhin; and then in the summer of 1945—while still living on to see the end of the war and the first few months of the rebirth of Europe—came the *Concerto No. 3* for piano and orchestra, which he wrote for his wife, Ditta Pásztory. Although he was rapidly getting weaker his spirit was unbroken and he succeeded in completing the orchestration of the *Concerto* with the exception of the last seventeen bars. However, there remain only a few sketches, with in places hardly decipherable notes, surviving of a *Concerto* for viola and orchestra which he had intended for William Primrose. These sketches were subsequently set down and orchestrated by the selfless labours of Tibor Serly who also on the basis of Bartók's notes completed the score of the final movement of the *Concerto No. 3* for piano and orchestra. Of the planned *String Quartet No. 7*, commissioned by Ralph Hawkes of the London firm of Boosey & Hawkes, he was able to put to paper only a few musical ideas. "I only regret that I have to depart with my luggage full," he said in his last days to one of the doctors treating him. He died on September 26, 1945, at the West Side Hospital in New York.

*

In 1905, a few months after his failure in Paris, Bartók who was then a follower of Nietzsche's wrote in sadness some fine words to his mother about the ups and downs of his mental make-up: "Sometimes I feel that for a brief space of time I have risen to these heights. Then comes a mighty crash; then again more struggle, always striving to rise higher; and this recurs again and again. The time may come when I shall be able to stay on the heights."

We have tried in these pages to devise a graph of these wave crests and wave throughs making up the course of Bartók's life, full as it was of crises and struggles—yet rising to heights indeed. This brief outline hardly does justice to the great works, important events and contemporaries playing significant roles in Bartók's life and indeed omits many. We have given an external and internal portrait, with the chief turning points in the development of the man and of the artist. But we repeat, we are not striving here to give a complete biography, only an introduction to that which is the principal part and purpose of this volume: the series of pictures and documents.

It is an open question whether these few hundred pictures are able to conjure up for us the figure of Bartók. The genuine story, the final meaning and truth of his life are hidden in the notes of his music. And yet, these pictures do record phases of his life, his work and his struggles: in this they are not without value. With the exception of the music reproduced here, they cannot illuminate the depth of his inner life. But they present him when young and old, with his family, his surroundings, his comrades-at-arms; they present the places where he lived, they document his human qualities, his manysided work, and those of his acts which could be preserved outside of pictorial means only by evanescent memory.

It is up to the reader, on whom Bartók's music has already left its mark, to reconstruct for himself a complete picture from this mosaic's hundred pieces.

PICTURES AND DOCUMENTS

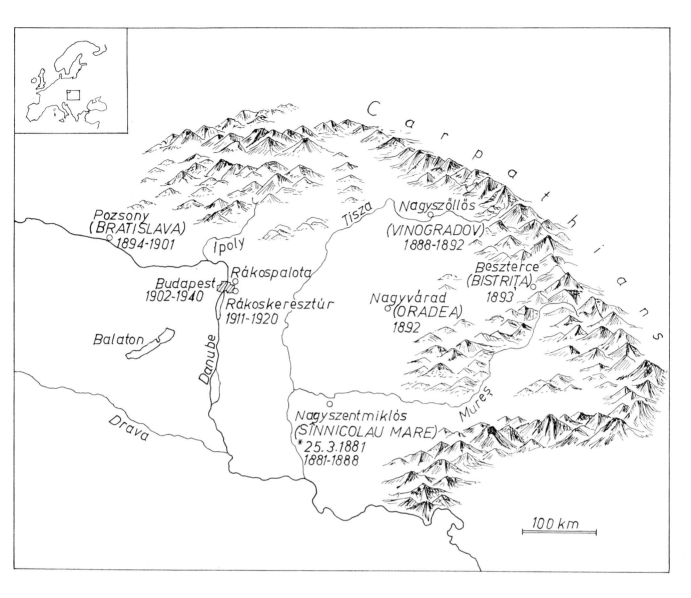

1 Béla Bartók's biographical map of Europe

2 JÁNOS BARTÓK (1817–1877), HEADMASTER OF AN AGRICULTURAL SCHOOL, THE COMPOSER'S GRANDFATHER

Research has been unable to trace the origin of the Bartók family back beyond the middle of the eighteenth century. The composer's great-great-grandfather was Gergely Bartók. He lived in Borsodszirák, northern Hungary, and had a son, János Bartók, who was a village notary in Magyarcsermely. His grandson— another János—was the first Bartók in Nagyszentmiklós (now Sînnicolau Mare, Rumania), the composer's native town.

3–4 Béla Bartók (1855–1888), headmaster of an agricultural school at Nagyszentmiklós (now Sînnicolau Mare, Rumania), the composer's father

He was an interesting and original personality, a broadminded man who was a leading figure in the cultural life of the small town. In addition to being a clever writer he was a good musician: he played the violoncello and was president of the Nagyszentmiklós Musical Society. The pictures of the composer's grandfather and father reveal a number of common family features. Particularly noteworthy is the singular, "Bartókian" contrast of calmness and tension on the two portraits of the father.

A contemporary—Pongrác Kacsóh—whom he met in her youth described her piano playing as follows: "...she played well, very well indeed; though performing was by no means her forte, her playing was pure, polished and, at the same time, feminine." From her did her son inherit his orderly and systematizing mind and his exactitude.

*(Photo by
F. L. Schnitzel)*

5 Mrs. Béla Bartók, née Paula Voit (1857–1939), was a school-teacher. She was the composer's mother and first piano teacher

Nagyszentmiklósi m. kir. földmives iskola főépülete (igazgatói lak.)

*Örvendtünk a sikerült aro képnek, köszönet érte.
Sok a dolgom, levélben legközelebb többet.*

903. VIII/18.

csókol: A.

6 THE NAGYSZENTMIKLÓS AGRICULTURAL SCHOOL

After the birth of their first child Béla on March 25, 1881, Bartók's parents moved here, where Béla spent the first seven years of his life. Soon after the untimely death of his father (August 4, 1888), his widowed mother, his younger sister and he were obliged to leave this house. His mother returned to school-teaching—which she had given up when she married—and though her salary was modest she managed on her own to bring up her son Béla and her daughter Elza.

It was in this house that Bartók's musical talent was first discovered. As his mother recalled, "When he was three, he was given a drum as a present, which he liked very much. When I was playing the piano, he sat on his little chair with the drum on a low stool in front of him. He kept beating the time accurately and when I changed from 3/4 to 4/4, he stopped beating the drum for a moment and then went on in the proper rhythm... When he was four years old he could play on the piano with one finger all the folk-songs he knew; he knew forty of them, and if we told him the first words of the text, he played the tune straight away."

7 BARTÓK'S BAPTISMAL CERTIFICATE

He was given the names Béla Viktor János after his father, godfather and grandfather.

In the year when Liszt, the greatest creative genius of nineteenth-century Hungarian music, died, Bartók was given his first piano lessons by his mother.

"...He was a frail child, but he begged me so insistently that I started teaching him all the same. But the lessons lasted half an hour or a quarter of an hour only. We began the lessons on March 25 (actually on his birthday), and on April 23, Béla Day, he surprised his father with playing a little piece for four hands."

(From his mother's reminiscences)

"...When he was three months old, right after the vaccination against smallpox... he broke out in a rash on his face... which later spread over the whole body. The poor child suffered very much... He was particularly tortured by itching at night and it was only after 6 a.m. that he could find some rest at last... He hid from people because he was hurt when they said, 'Poor little Béla!' ... This rash pestered him until his fifth year..."

(From his mother's reminiscences)

Nagy-Szőllős.

10 NAGYSZŐLLŐS (NOW VINOGRADOV, CARPATHO-UKRAINE, USSR)

"...In 1889 we got to Nagyszőllős, where I was given a job as a school-teacher; it was a small place and did not have any musical life, thus he had no musical nourishment and I continued teaching him according to my modest abilities. One afternoon, when he was nine, I was asleep in the adjoining room, a melody was taking shape in his mind, one he had never played and never heard before. He could not play it on the piano, for fear of waking me. But when I awoke, he told me about it. He played it to me at once, and it was a valse, entirely different from anything he had heard before. From then on he composed dance tunes and other pieces in quick succession..."

(From his mother's reminiscences)

11 FIRST PAGE OF "THE COURSE OF THE DANUBE", THE MOST FAMOUS OF HIS CHILDHOOD COMPOSITIONS

Inspired by his geography lessons, Bartók composed this long (20 minutes) piece when he was ten years old. The music follows the course of the Danube from its source to the sea. The river greets Hungary at Dévény with a merry tune ("Polka. It is jubilant, for it has come to Hungary"), and strikes a sad note when it leaves the country at the Iron Gate.

Hangverseny. A helybeli polg. iskola ifjusága a szegény tanulók segély-alapja javára f. hó 1-én egy sikerült hang-versenyt adott. A közönség szép számmal jelent meg s igy mintegy 50 frt tiszta jö-vedelem folyt a szegény tanulók kasszájába. Azonban határozottan nagyobb volt az elért siker erkölcsi tekintetben; a dalok mind igen jól adattak elő, a közönség többször meg is ujrázta; a tavasz ébredése és a talpra magyar egészen elragadta a kö-zönséget. Az ének darabokban ki kell emelni Lövy Róza IV. osztályos tanulót, ki a kis sereg primadonnája volt, aratott sok, jól kiérdemelt tapsokat. De mindezeknél még nagyobb mértékben magára vonta a közön-ség figyelmét a kis Bartók Béla II-od osztályos gyimnasiumi tanuló, ki zongora müvészetét bemutatandó, vendégszerepelni jött N. Szöllősre. Az előadott klassikus da-rabok a legnagyobb kézi ügyességre valla-nak s hogy a zongora müvészetre a 10 éves fiunak nagy hivatottsága van, ketscgen kivüi elárulta az eljátszott darabokkal. A fiatal genie kompositiójából is bemutatott egy darabot, „A Duna folyását", mely szintén sok tapsot nyert. A kis Bartók Béla első nyilvános fellépése alkalmából kapott több diszes csokrot. Méltó elismerés illeti meg Nagy Gábor karmestert és énektanárt, valamint Mihalik József urat, kik fáradha-tatlan buzgósággal müködtek közre az est sikerében.

12–13 BARTÓK'S DEBUT BEFORE THE PUBLIC RECORDED IN THE MAY 8, 1892 ISSUE OF THE NAGYSZŐLLŐS PAPER "UGOCSA"

The recital took place on May 1, 1892. Bartók, who was eleven at the time, was one of the performers at a charity concert; he played several pieces including the first movement of Beethoven's Waldstein Sonata and then concluded the programme with his own composition, *The Course of the Danube*—a world première. As recorded by his proud mother, "There was a storm of applause, he got seven nosegays, one of them being most cleverly made up from sweets."

14 Bartók and his sister, four years his junior, in Pozsony (now Bratislava, Czechoslovakia), in 1892, the year of the première of "The Course of the Danube"

(Photo by Mindszenty)

15–16 Nagyvárad (now Oradea, Rumania)

Here, in 1891–92, Bartók lived with his widowed aunt, Mrs. Lajos Voit, in the four-windowed house shown in the foreground (his window was the one on the right). He completed the second form at the grammar school (the two-storey building) shown in the bottom of the photograph, but disliked it there because as we know from his mother, the masters "only liked the children of wealthy parents, boys who had tutors; they treated the others unjustly."

17 FERENC KERSCH (1853–1910)

Bartók's piano teacher at Nagyvárad "under whom he studied a great number of pieces, but somewhat superficially. He made him learn too difficult pieces; he liked to show off with him and was glad if he learned some rather difficult piece within a week; that such a result could not be perfect is only natural."

(From his mother's reminiscences)

18 LÁSZLÓ ERKEL (1844–1896)

Son of Ferenc Erkel, the creator of Hungarian national opera. While a grammar-school student in Pozsony, Bartók studied piano and musical theory under him for several years. During this time Bartók "composed all the time; however, it was no longer dance music but more serious pieces."

(From his mother's reminiscences)

19 Pozsony

The town where he spent most of his grammar-school years (1892–93; 1894–99). It was here that he first composed songs and chamber music.

20 Bartók at fourteen with his sister in Pozsony, 1895

(Photo by Sándor Fink)

21 With his class-mates at the Pozsony grammar school, 1899

(Bartók is on the far right in the second row from the top.) He gave his first public performance in Pozsony in 1896, accompanying on the piano a recitation in the theatre. In 1897 he gave a successful performance of Liszt's *Spanish Rhapsody*, and in the following year of Tausig's *Rhapsody* and of Wagner's *Tannhäuser Overture* transcribed for the piano.

22 Béla Bartók's grammar-school graduation picture, Pozsony, 1899

In the autumn of the same year—a few days after he signed the photograph—he went to Budapest and gained admission to the departments of piano and composition at the Academy of Music.

(Photo by Marian, Pozsony)

42

23–24 BUDAPEST, ABOUT 1900

Above: The Tabán District of Buda, the Royal Palace and the Chain Bridge; in the background, on the Pest side, the Parliament.
Below: Andrássy Avenue, where the old Academy of Music used to stand and where the Opera House stands even to this day. Bartók had lodgings for a time in Andrássy Avenue while studying at the Academy.

25 ÖDÖN MIHALOVICH (1842–1929)

For thirty-two years Mihalovich was the director of the Academy of Music in Budapest (1887–1919). It was he who admitted Bartók to the Academy following his nomination by István Thomán. "...The director warmly clasped both my hands and congratulated me upon my son's talent; he had been admitted to the second year of the Academy"—thus Bartók's mother recalls this notable day in September 1899.

26 THE ACADEMY OF MUSIC ON ANDRÁSSY AVENUE, BUDAPEST, WHERE BARTÓK COMPLETED HIS STUDIES IN MUSIC (1899–1903)

The second-floor balcony belonged to the apartment of Franz Liszt, the first President of the Academy. To its right are three windows of the organ and concert hall.

27 LISZT'S NAME-PLATE ON THE DOOR OF HIS APARTMENT IN THE BUDAPEST ACADEMY OF MUSIC

28 THE ORGAN AND CONCERT HALL OF THE ACADEMY OF MUSIC ON ANDRÁSSY AVENUE

The door to the right of the platform led to Liszt's apartment. In this hall Bartók made his first appearance before the audiences of the Hungarian capital.

29 ISTVÁN THOMÁN (1862–1941)

Bartók studied the piano at the Academy of Music in Budapest under this former pupil of Liszt. An intimate friendship developed later between Thomán and Bartók. In 1903 Bartók dedicated a piece for the piano entitled *Study for the Left Hand* "To his master, István Thomán". "I learned particularly much from Thomán in the interpretation of Chopin and Liszt," Bartók recalled in 1927. "In playing Beethoven I was striving, from the beginning, for individual ideals, ideals Thomán never tried to suppress in me, for he was one of those rare teachers who never suppress their pupils' personalities."

30 HANS KOESSLER (1853–1926)

Bartók's professor of composition at the Academy of Music. He was a great admirer of Brahms and taught in his spirit. Though he was convinced that it was impossible to create independent Hungarian composed music, the most significant masters of twentieth-century Hungarian music were developed by him: in addition to Bartók, there were Zoltán Kodály, Leó Weiner, Ernst von Dohnányi and the there famous composers of the Hungarian operetta: Emmerich Kálmán, Victor Jacobi and Albert Sirmay.

31 István Thomán's class in 1901

Standing first on the left is Arnold Székely, later a
renowned concert pianist and teacher; third is Bartók
and fourth Sári Erkel, grand-daughter of Ferenc
Erkel; tenth is the composer and conductor Emil
Ábrányi Jr., who later became director of the Budapest Opera House. Seated second on the right is
Felicitas Fábián, one of the idols of Bartók's young
years.

32 THE PROGRAMME OF BARTÓK'S FIRST PERFORMANCE IN
BUDAPEST

On the Academy of Music's fourth house concert,
held on March 31, 1900, in the Academy organ and
concert hall, Bartók played the first movement of
Beethoven's *Piano Concerto* in C Minor, accompanied
on the second piano by his master, István Thomán.

33–34 In 1901

About this period Bartók himself wrote that as a composer he practically did not work at all and was only known at the Academy as an excellent pianist.

In the upper picture he is sitting with his mother and his sister Elza in the garden of the Budapest home of his widowed aunt Mrs. Lajos Voit. Standing behind them are his cousin Ervin Voit and Gyula Chorus, a student at the Technical University.

35–36 IN 1901

In the summer of 1900 Bartók was seriously ill with pneumonia and pleurisy. One of his doctors abandoned hope for his life, but careful nursing and several months' rest at the mountain resort of Meran restored his health. It was not until the spring of 1901 that he was able to return home and resume his studies at the Academy of Music.

37 "Békés Kunyhó"

The Bartók family spent the summer of 1901 in this villa near Pozsony. It was here that Bartók prepared himself for the autumn performance of Liszt's *Sonata* in B Minor.
In front of Bartók is seated his mother with his aunt ("Aunt Irma") to her right. Bartók's younger sister Elza is on the right-hand side of the picture; to the composer's left is his cousin Lajos Voit ("Lujcsi").

38 Lunch-time in Pozsony, summer 1901

From left to right, the composer, his sister Elza, Aunt Irma and his mother.
In front of the composer, recently recovered from a grave illness, stands the "medicine": a glass of fresh milk.

39 "THE PUPIL PRACTISED..."

A page from István Thomán's Academy of Music record and attendance book. The entries are in Bartók's own hand and list the pieces he had learned during the school-year of 1901–1902.

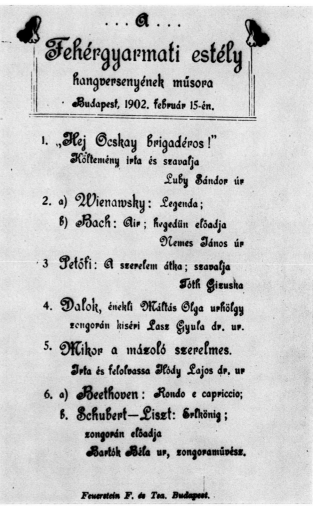

40 "...PERFORMED BY MR. BÉLA BARTÓK, CONCERT PIANIST"

Most of the performers at this Budapest concert would seem from the programme to have been amateurs, with Bartók probably the only professional among them. He played two pieces he had recently studied at the Academy of Music.

41 In 1902

Bartók returned from Meran, where—to quote Kodály—"he put on so much weight that characterology may have grouped him with the picnic type." During this year, under the impact of the Budapest première of Richard Strauss's symphonic poem *Thus Spake Zoroaster*, he tried his hand at composing again.

(Photo by Uher, Budapest)

52

42 MRS. EMMA GRUBER NÉE SÁNDOR

In 1910 Mrs. Emma Gruber married Zoltán Kodály and was his wife until her death in 1958. A woman of extraordinary talent and culture: she was a pianist, composer and folk-song collector. For a time, beginning in 1902, she studied counterpoint under Bartók. At the turn of the century her home was a centre of new trends in music: it was there that Bartók and Kodály started their lifelong friendship.

43 ONE OF THE SLOVAK PIECES OF BARTÓK'S WORK "FOR CHILDREN": MRS. GRUBER'S ARRANGEMENT AND HANDWRITING

Ernst von Dohnányi wrote variations on a theme by Mrs. Emma Gruber and Bartók published under his own name two of her folk-song arrangements as part of his series *For Children*.

One of the variations of Kodály's *First String Quartet* was also her composition. Bartók dedicated to her his *Fantasy No. 1* for piano (1903) and his *Rhapsody* for piano (op. 1, 1904).

53

On July 2, 1903, the Budapest theatre and music weekly *Zenevilág* (The World of Music) devoted a leading article to the 22-year-old Bartók. According to the article: "The purpose and task of these lines is to draw the attention of the cultured and music-loving Hungarian public to the phenomenal young genius, whose name is today only known to few, but who—and this is our firm belief—is destined to play a great and brilliant role in the history of Hungarian music."

45 "FOUR SONGS", 1902

The earliest of Bartók's compositions to be published during his lifetime. The *Four Songs* set poems by Lajos Pósa to music; they were composed while Bartók was still studying at the Academy of Music and published in 1904 by Ferenc Bárd and Brother, Budapest.

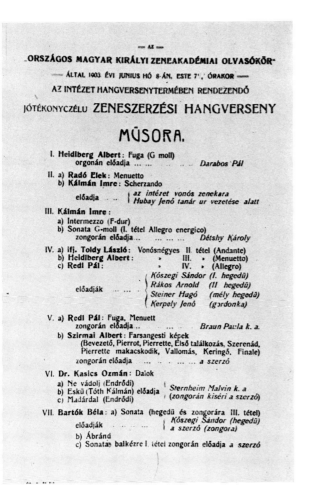

46–48 BUDAPEST–BERLIN–VIENNA

In 1903 Bartók completed his studies at the Academy of Music. On January 26 of that year he appeared at a concert of the Tonkünstlerverein in Vienna, playing his own piano-transcription of Richard Strauss's symphonic poem *Ein Heldenleben*. On April 13 he gave his first recital at Nagyszentmiklós, his native town. His first piano recital abroad took place in Berlin on December 14, and his first chamber-music performance abroad in Vienna on February 3, 1904.

49 WINTER 1903–1904: THE COMPOSER OF THE SYMPHONIC POEM "KOSSUTH"

In Bowdon, on February 26, 1904, Bartók dedicated this photograph to Hans Richter, who conducted the Manchester première of the composition. The music shown is the beginning of *Fantasy No. 1.*

(*Photo by Mai and Co., Budapest*)

50 "Down with the Habsburgs!"

Letter-head from 1903.

51 "Kossuth"

Analysis by Bartók of the symphonic poem he composed in 1903, together with a parody of the Austrian imperial anthem.

In addition to Strauss's influence "other circumstances entered my life at the same time which proved a decisive influence on my development. It was the time of a new national movement in Hungary, which also took hold of art and music. In music, too, the aim was set to create something specifically Hungarian. When this movement reached me, it drew my attention to studying Hungarian folk music, or, to be more exact, what at time was considered Hungarian folk music. Under these diverse influences I composed in 1903 a symphonic poem entitled Kossuth..."

(From Bartók's Autobiography)

First page of the symphonic poem's fair copy score as corrected by Bartók, and the German programme notes he wrote for it.

"The year 1848 is one of the most eventful in Hungarian history. It was the year of the Hungarian revolt—a life and death struggle of the nation for freedom. The leader, the heart and soul of this struggle, was Louis Kossuth."

(From the English draft of the programme notes for the symphonic poem Kossuth)

54 The orchestra of the Budapest Philharmonic Society with president-conductor István Kerner (1867–1929)

This photograph was taken in 1903—the year Bartók composed the symphonic poem *Kossuth* on the occasion of the orchestra's fiftieth anniversary.

(Photo by Strelisky, Budapest)

55 Programme of the Budapest Philharmonic Society concert conducted by István Kerner on January 13, 1904

This was the première of Bartók's symphonic poem *Kossuth*. As a result of this composition the 23-year-old Bartók gained nation-wide fame overnight.

"After the Wednesday philharmonic concert Bartók has become unquestionably the first and foremost composer of Hungary," wrote the Budapest weekly *Zenevilág*.

56 THE FREE TRADE HALL IN MANCHESTER

where Bartók, composer and pianist, first appeared before English audiences.

THE HALLÉ CONCERTS SOCIETY.

Forty-Sixth Season.

SIXTEENTH CONCERT,

Thursday, February 18th, 1904.

✿

PROGRAMME.

Part I.

SYMPHONY, No. 8, in B minor - "Unfinished" - Schubert.

SPANISH RHAPSODY (orchestrated by F. Busoni) - Liszt.
(First time at these Concerts.)
Mr. BÉLA BARTÓK.

AN INTERVAL OF FIFTEEN MINUTES.

Part II.

SYMPHONIC POEM - "Kossuth" - - - - Béla Bartók.
(First time at these Concerts.)

VARIATIONS on a Theme by Handel - - - - Volkmann.
(First time at these Concerts.)
Mr. BÉLA BARTÓK.

SUITE for Orchestra (Op. 39) - - - - - Dvořák.

✿

Conductor - - Dr HANS RICHTER.

57 THE SYMPHONIC POEM "KOSSUTH"

was performed in Manchester scarcely a month after its world première in Budapest.
It was played on February 18, 1904, by the Hallé Orchestra, under the baton of Hans Richter.
At the same concert Bartók himself played compositions of Volkmann and Liszt.

60

58 A Vienna portrait from 1904, with Bartók's dedication dated 1905

The music: the opening theme of his *Suite No. 1* for orchestra.

(István Vedrődy-Vogyeraczky's painting)

Bartók analysed this composition in the programme notes he wrote for its première, which was conducted by Ferdinand Löwe in Vienna on November 29, 1905. At the same concert Hans Pfitzner and Siegfried Wagner each conducted one of his own compositions.

1905 was the decisive year in Bartók's career: he failed to win the Rubinstein Competition in Paris and as a result turned his full attention to composition.

61 Bartók, Lajos Vecsey and violinist Ferenc Vecsey in Spain, spring 1906

62 The programme of the Porto concerts given by Vecsey and Bartók on April 8 and 10, 1906

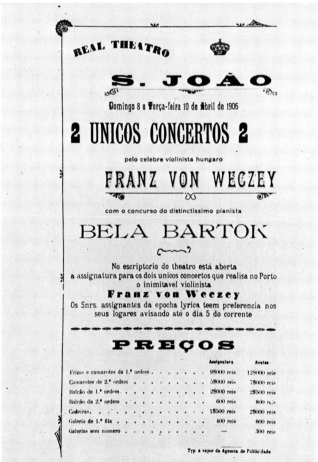

Bartók toured Spain and Portugal in the spring of 1906 as accompanist for violinist Ferenc Vecsey.

63

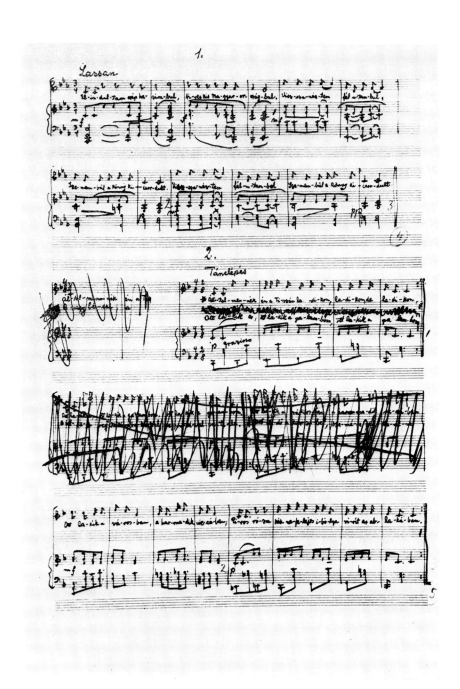

63 "Hungarian Folk-Songs" for voice and piano (1906)

(Copyright by Editio Musica Budapest)

From the viewpoint of Hungarian musical history, the most important event of the year 1906 was the appearance of a collection of *Hungarian Folk-Songs*, containing ten of Bartók's and ten of Kodály's arrangements.
"I discovered that what we had known as Hungarian folk-songs till then were more or less trivial songs by popular composers and did not contain much that was valuable. I felt an urge to go deeper into this question and set out in 1905 to collect and study Hungarian peasant music unknown until then. It was my great good luck to find a helpmate for this work in Zoltán Kodály, who, owing to his deep insight and sound judgement in all spheres of music, could give me many a hint and much advice that proved of immense value."

(From Bartók's Autobiography)

64 Bartók, Professor of the Academy of Music (1907)

In 1907, the year the new building in Liszt Ferenc Square was inaugurated, Bartók was appointed Professor of piano at the Academy.
In addition to teaching in this building, Bartók gave a number of recitals in its concert hall, including his last European concert which took place on October 8, 1940.

65 The Ferenc Liszt Academy of Music in Budapest

From this trip "he re-
turned with such a host
of pentatonic tunes that
when comparing them
with those I had collect-
ed in the North, the
basic importance of this
scale, which had been
unnoticed before, be-
came evident at once."

*(Kodály:
"Bartók, the Folklorist")*

*(Photo by István Kováts,
Gyergyószentmiklós)*

During his Transylvanian tour Bartók informed his mother that he had a peasant joiner from Körösfő (now Crișeni, Rumania) make the furniture for his new home and that the pieces were already on their way to the capital.

67 GREETING FROM BÁNFFYHUNYAD (NOW HUEDIN, RUMANIA)

68 A PAGE FROM THE NOTEBOOK IN WHICH BARTÓK COLLECTED FOLK MUSIC

The pentatonic tune in the bottom line—"Snow-white kerchief, dark both field and furrow show"—was subsequently published by Bartók as the first piece in the cycle entitled *Eight Hungarian Folk-Songs*.

69 Bartók in 1908 collecting Slovak folk-songs in the village of Darázs, in Nyitra County (now Drazovce, Czecho-slovakia)

"From the very beginning Bartók had been aware that without the knowledge of the music of the neighbouring peoples one could not really know Hungarian music either. And since their collections were next to nothing this task too devolved upon us."

(Kodály: "Bartók, the Folklorist")

70 A Slovak folk-song from Bartók's notebook

The "source" of one of the Slovak pieces in the piano composition *For Children*.

71 "For Children"

Dated 1908, this four-volume piano composition is the first in which Bartók speaks to the musicians of the future. The work is an arrangement, masterly in its simplicity, of Hungarian and Slovak folk-songs.

72 A Hungarian folk-song collected in 1907

Arranged for the piano it became popular as piece No. 17 in the first volume of *For Children*.

73 Violinist Stefi Geyer (1888–1956)

She attracted attention while still a young pupil of Jenő Hubay's at the Budapest Academy of Music. From the twenties on she lived in Switzerland. The letters Bartók wrote to her around 1907 indicate that he was deeply in love with her—but his love was unrequited.

The young violinist dedicated this photo to her friend Mici Lukács, younger sister of the Hungarian philosopher Georg Lukács.

74 "First Violin Concerto"

Draft of the concerto composed in 1907–08 for Stefi Geyer, with the composer's amusing drawings and remarks about the orchestration ("thickly, growling Bang! bang! bang! bang! bang!").

The work was first performed in 1958, after the death of both the composer and the violinist.

75 In the garden of the Park Hotel at Vitznau

During his first trip to Switzerland in 1908, Bartók visited pianist Robert Freund and his family. Among them Etelka Freund, Robert Freund's sister, who was one of the earliest admirers of Bartók's music.

(Photo by Irma Hercz-Freund)

76 Bartók playing the hurdy-gurdy in his new home on Teréz Boulevard in Budapest, June 1908

77 With the new furniture from Körösfő

78–80 "FOURTEEN BAGATELLES" OP. 6

(Copyright by Editio Musica Budapest)

This cycle, composed in 1908, permits some insight into Bartók's work methods. The first piece (above left) is bitonal and explores methods of applying two tonalities simultaneously. The second Bagatelle (above right) is an experiment with "tonal chromaticism", its theme comprising eleven different tones. The fifth piece (bottom right) investigates the possibilities of form and harmony offered by the Hungarian folk-song.

81 WITH ZOLTÁN KODÁLY IN 1908

82 THE SIXTH OF THE "FOURTEEN BAGATELLES"
IN BARTÓK'S HANDWRITING

(Copyright by Editio Musica Budapest)

83 "...I appreciate Kodály as the best Hungarian musician not because he is my friend; indeed, he became my only friend because (apart from his excellent human qualities) he is the best Hungarian musician."

(Bartók: "Zoltán Kodály", 1921)

84 KODÁLY'S COPY OF THE SIXTH BAGATELLE

(Copyright by Editio Musica Budapest)

Bartók performed the work first in the summer of 1908 in Busoni's master-class for piano in Vienna.

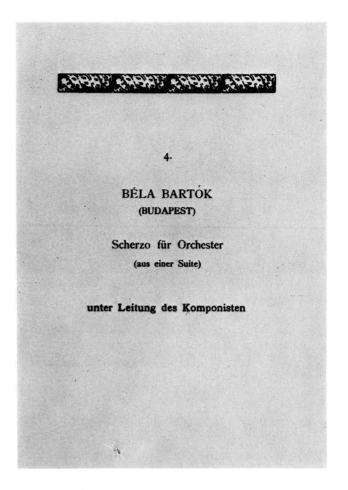

85–86 THE PROGRAMME OF THE ONLY CONCERT BARTÓK EVER CONDUCTED

On January 2, 1909, at the invitation of Ferruccio Busoni, an important patron of new music, Bartók conducted the Berlin Philharmonic Orchestra in the Scherzo movement of his *Suite No. 2* for orchestra. This was his first and only appearance as a conductor.

87 WITH HIS PUPIL IN COMPOSITION IN 1909

Composer and writer on music Gisela Selden-Goth.

88–89 "Portrait of a girl"...

(Copyright by Editio Musica Budapest)

The first piece of Bartók's piano composition *Seven Sketches* op. 9b. It was dedicated "to Márta, 1908".

90 ...and the "model"

Márta Ziegler, whom Bartók married in 1909.

(Photo by Zoltán Kodály)

91 THE BLOCK OF FLATS ON TERÉZ BOULEVARD

One of the busiest spots in Budapest, near the Academy of Music. It was in this building—in the corner-flat on the top floor—that Bartók lived at the time of his marriage.

(Photo by Gyula Kertész)

92 BARTÓK THE COLLECTOR...

His cousin Ervin Voit's water-colour of Bartók, the passionate collector of insects.

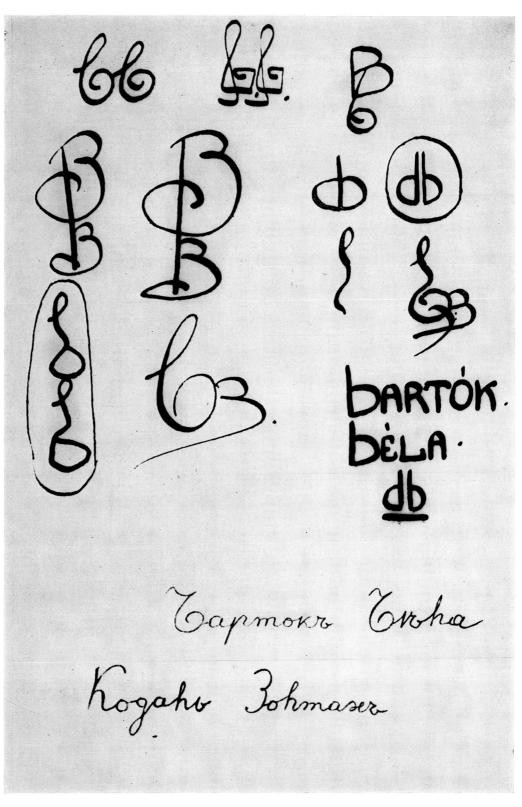

93 . . . AND THE "VARIATOR"

His own variations on his initials. At the bottom of the page: the names Béla Bartók and Zoltán Kodály written by Bartók in Cyrillic characters.

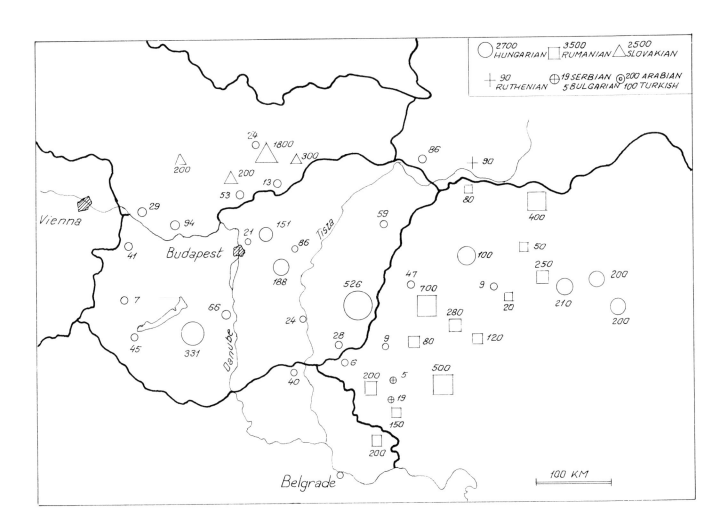

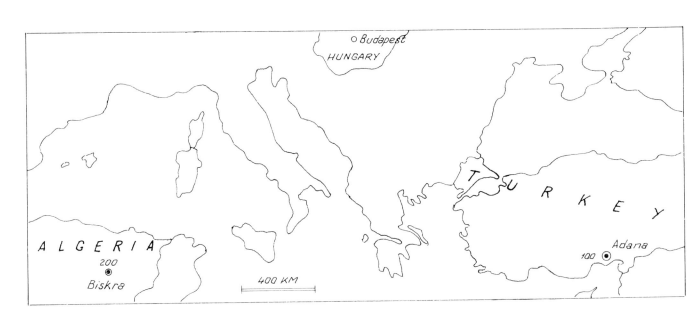

94 THE MAPS OF BARTÓK'S FOLK-SONG COLLECTING TOURS

A Rumanian folk-song jotted down on a postcard sent by Bartók to István Thomán. "I started these investigations on entirely musical grounds and pursued them in areas which linguistically were purely Hungarian. Later I became fascinated by the scientific implications of my musical material and extended my work over territories which were linguistically Slovakian and Rumanian."

(From Bartók's Autobiography)

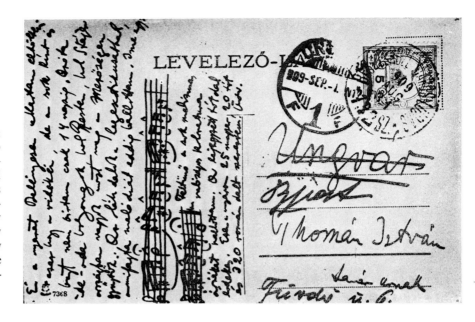

96 "FIRST RUMANIAN DANCE"

(Copyright by Editio Musica Budapest)

Though this 1910 piano piece was inspired by Rumanian folk music, it is not a folk-song arrangement but an original composition of Bartók's.

His criticism of the Budapest première of Richard Strauss's *Elektra* reflects his disappointment and disillusionment. "There are hardly any ideas in it hitherto unfelt, unheard and unexpressed... ...how can someone who is able to say so many interesting things get to so shallow, 'half-hearted... *Kapellmeister*-music' when expressing exalted feelings..."

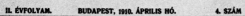

II. ÉVFOLYAM.   BUDAPEST, 1910. ÁPRILIS HÓ.   4. SZÁM.

A ZENE

ZENEMŰVÉSZETI HAVI FOLYÓIRAT.

| Szerkesztőség és kiadóhivatal: | Szerkesztik: | Előfizetési ára: Egy évre 4 kor. |
| Budapest, VIII., Szentkirályi-u. 1a. | Sereghy Elemér és Luria Arthur | Egyes szám ára 40 fillér. |

Elektra.

Strauss Richard operája. Bemutató előadása a m. kir. operaházban 1910. március 11-én.

Salome után *Elektra*: csalódás. Minden új munka megkezdésénél jóformán meg kellene feledkezni az előbbiekről, nehogy valamiképen önutánzásba kerüljünk. Megint — újra vártam Elektránál, de hiába. Alig akad benne eddig még nem érzett, nem hallott, ki nem fejezett gondolat, ami arra ösztökélne, hogy megkívánjam a megismétlést, akár hallva, akár olvasva. Az egészet amolyan átlag Strauss-nak mondanám. Igaz ugyan, hogy Straussban, mint mai legjobb zeneszerzőink egyikében, már az átlagos sem egészen érdektelen. De ennél sokkal többet kell kivánnunk: azt, aminek megírásához magasabb inspiráció kell. És éppen ebben *Salome* sokkal nagyobb. Ott már a kezdő jelenetek poézise, Herodes nagy jelenete, a zsidók kvintettje mindmegannyi új szín, értékes kép. Viszont Elektrában már a bekezdő jelenetek töredezettsége fárasztó; a folytatódás se nagyon bíztató. Talán a legérdekesebb: Klytämnestra nagy jelenete. Egy valamit azonban sem ebben, sem egyéb Straussban sehogysem értek: hogyan juthat valaki, aki annyi érdekeset tud mondani, u. n. fenkölt érzelmek kifejezésénél anynyira sekély „lagymatag", „Kapellmeister"-zenébe (pl. Elektra határtalan öröme Orestes megérkeztén végnélküli *as*-durban, a legközönségesebb eszközökkel fejeződik ki) ilyesmi százszámra található Strauss műveiben. A kérdés már mostan az, amire

Közleményeink csakis a forrás megnevezésével vehetők át.

98 PARIS, MARCH 12, 1910

Programme of the Hungarian concert held in Paris at which Bartók appeared both as composer and pianist. Some critics labelled him and Kodály "young barbarians".

FESTIVAL HONGROIS

donné
Le Samedi 12 Mars, à 9 heures
A L'HOTEL DES MODES, 15, RUE DE LA VILLE-L'ÉVÊQUE

PAR

ŐDÖN MIHALOVICH   BÉLA BARTÓK
ÁRPÁD SZENDY   ZOLTÁN KODÁLY
ERNŐ DOHNÁNYI   LEÓ VÁNDOR-WEINER

AVEC LE CONCOURS DE

Mlle TRELLI

ET DE

MM. GÁBRIEL, FRANCESCHI, MIHALKOVICS, SÁNDOR KOVÁCS

Causerie de M. HENRY EXPERT

PROGRAMME

I. LEÓ VÁNDOR-WEINER, Professeur au Conservatoire de Budapest.
   TRIO POUR CORDES
   a. Allegro con brio. — b. Vivace. — c. Andante. — d. Allegro con fuoco.
   MM. GÁBRIEL, FRANCESCHI, MIHALKOVICS

II. ÁRPÁD SZENDY, Professeur au Conservatoire de Budapest.
    APHORISMES Nos 4, 6, 7, 9, 10
    Joués au piano par M. BÉLA BARTÓK, Prof. au Conservatoire de Budapest.

III. ZOLTÁN KODÁLY, Professeur au Conservatoire de Budapest.
     SONATE POUR VIOLONCELLE ET PIANO (1er et 2e parties)

IV. BÉLA BARTÓK.
    a. 1) BAGATELLES. b. FANTAISIE. c. DANSE ROUMAINE (manuscrit).

V. ŐDÖN MIHALOVICH, Directeur du Conservatoire de Budapest.
   TROIS MÉLODIES
   Mlle TRELLI, accompagnée par M. SÁNDOR KOVÁCS

VI. ERNŐ DOHNÁNYI, Professeur à la Haute École de Musique de Berlin.
    TRIO POUR CORDES
    a. — Marcia. — b. Romanza. — c. Scherzo. — d. Tema con variazioni. — e. Rondo.
    MM. GÁBRIEL, FRANCESCHI, MIHALKOVICS

PIANO ÉRARD

99 "ALLEGRO BARBARO"

This work was both Bartók's answer to his Paris critics and the first mature example of the fast-paced style which was inspired by the passionate rhythms and indomitable energy of folk-dance music.

100 IN 1910

The year of his first public concert in Paris and the first all-Bartók night in Budapest.

101 Bartók, Kodály and the Waldbauer–Kerpely String Quartet, March 1910

Seated, from left to right: Bartók, Antal Molnár (viola), Kodály, Jenő Kerpely ('cello). Standing: János Temesváry (second violin) and Imre Waldbauer (first violin).
The Waldbauer–Kerpely String Quartet was formed especially for the world première of Kodály's and Bartók's first string quartets. It took them 90 to 100 rehearsals to prepare the two concerts held in Budapest on March 17, 1910 (all Kodály) and March 19 (all Bartók).

(Photo by Aladár Székely)

102 Béla Balázs (1884–1949)

Writer and film aesthetician, who wrote the libretti for Bartók's opera and ballet as well as for Kodály's stage composition *Czinka Panna*. In fact, it was Balázs's highly original themes, combining folk-tale elements and ballads with a modern psychological approach, which drew Bartók to the stage.

103 3 Jókai Street at Rákoskeresztúr

In 1911 Bartók and his family moved to this quiet garden
suburb of Budapest.
They lived there for a year, next door to violinist Ferenc Vecsey
and his family.

(Photo by Gyula Kertész)

104 In Kodály's home, 1912

105 THE WINDOW OF BARTÓK'S STUDY IN THE JÓKAI STREET HOUSE

(Photo by Gyula Kertész)

It was here that he completed his opera *Bluebeard's Castle* in the summer of 1911.

106 "BLUEBEARD'S CASTLE"

(Copyright by Universal Edition A. G. Wien)

The original manuscript of Bartók's first composition for the stage.
Mrs. Emma Kodály's German translation of the text written on the manuscript by her and Kodály together,

CSÜTÖRTÖKÖN, E HÓ 18=ÁN ESTE PONTBAN HÉT ÓRAKOR A
"NYOLCAK" KÉPKIÁLLITÁSUKON AZ ERZSÉBET=
TÉRI "NEMZETI SZALON="BAN BARTÓK
BÉLA, KERPELY JENŐ, WALDBAUER
IMRE, MOLNÁR ANTAL ÉS TEMESVÁRY
JÁNOS URAK KÖZREMŰKÖDÉSÉVEL
BARTÓK BÉLA, KODÁLY ZOLTÁN ÉS
WEINER LEÓ MŰVEIBŐL

HANGVERSENYT

RENDEZNEK, MELYRE KÉRJÜK SZÍVES
MEGJELENÉSÉT.

PALLAS R.-T.
NYOMDÁJA
BUDAPEST.

JEGYEK KAPHATÓK:
RÓZSAVÖLGYI ÉS TÁRSA UDVARI ZENEMŰKERESKE-
DÉSÉBEN ÉS A NEMZETI SZALON PÉNZTÁRÁNÁL.

107–108 Bartók at the Group of "Eight" concert

On May 18, 1911, Bartók and the Waldbauer–Kerpely
String Quartet took part in a concert given in Budapest
at the exhibition of the Group of "Eight", a society of
progressive artists. At this concert Bartók first presented *A bit tipsy* to the public; this piece was the second of
his *Three Burlesques* op. 8c, a new series for piano
which was published in 1912.
The title-page of the composition was designed by
Bartók's cousin Ervin Voit.

109 28 Teréz Street, Rákoskeresztúr which became Bartók's home in 1912

(Photo by Gyula Kertész)

"In 1911... a number of young musicians, Kodály and myself among them, tried hard to found a New Hungarian Musical Union. The chief aim of the new organization would have been to form an orchestra able to perform old, new and recent music in a proper way. But we strove in vain, we could not achieve our aim. Other more personal disappointments were added to this broken plan and in 1912 I retired completely from public life. With more enthusiasm than ever I devoted myself to studies in musical folklore."

(From Bartók's Autobiography)

110 The composer in 1912 after his withdrawal from public musical life

90

111 A TRIP TO THE REGION FROM WHICH BARTÓK'S CARVED FURNITURE HAD COME

With Kodály and his wife in Körösfő church, 1912.

112 "WITH MORE ENTHUSIASM THAN EVER I DEVOTED MYSELF TO STUDIES IN MUSICAL FOLKLORE"

A page from the notebook in which he wrote down the folk-songs he had collected and recorded on the phonograph in 1912. Bartók later revised this version of the song several times. Arranged for voice and piano it became the nineteenth song in the cycle *Twenty Hungarian Folk-Songs* which Bartók composed in 1929.

113–114 ARNOLD SCHOENBERG'S LETTER TO BARTÓK, MAY 7, 1912

Arnold Schönberg, Berlin–Zehlendorf–Wannseebahn   7/5. 1912
     Machnower Chaussee, Villa Lepcke.

"Sehr geehrter Herr, es war ursprünglich die Absicht der österreichischen Wiener Musikfest-
woche, die nur tote Komponisten vorführt ein Gegenstück unter dem Titel 'Musikfest der
unofficiellen österreichischen Tonkunst' entgegenzusetzen. Dieses sollte Werke modernster
österreichischer (deutscher, ungarischer und tschechischer Nation) Komponisten in womög-
lich 2–3 Konzerten bringen. Dazu sollten die Ungarn und die Czechen Beiträge leisten und
jene Autoren des modernsten Stils namhaft machen, die sie bei dieser Gelegenheit aufführen
wollten. Nun haben, wie ich gehört habe die Czechen zwar ihre moralische Unterstützung
bis jetzt zugesagt, noch *nicht* aber die financielle, während Ihre Landsleute unter Hinweis
auf eigene Konzerte, die im Herbst in Wien mit ungarischer Musik gegeben werden sollen,
abgelehnt.
Ich sende Ihren Brief nach Wien von wo man Ihnen eventuell schreiben wird. Falls Sie mei-
nen die Unterstützung seitens Ihrer Landsleute durchsetzen zu können, so bitte ich Sie das
mir oder direkt an Herrn Ingenieur Paul Königer (Wien XIII. Kuppelwieserstr 27) zu schreiben. Mit vorzüglicher Hochachtung Arnold Schönberg"

In the years following 1910 Bartók and Schoenberg were very interested in each other's works. Bartók ordered several of
Schoenberg's published works or studied them in manuscript copies. In 1920 he wrote the article "Arnold Schönbergs
Musik in Ungarn" for the Vienna periodical *Musikblätter des Anbruch*, and in 1922 he played Schoenberg's works as well
as his own at the Sorbonne in Paris. As early as 1911 Schoenberg referred to one of Bartók's compositions in his book on
harmonics. Later he was head of the Vienna Verein für Musikalische Privataufführungen which performed seven
compositions by Bartók between 1918 and 1920.

115–116 In Berlin in the summer of 1912

This year was one of the most critical periods in Bartók's life. His letter to Géza Vilmos Zágon dated August 22nd, 1913 reveals the following: "… a year ago sentence of death was officially pronounced on me as a composer. Either those people are right, in which case I am an untalented bungler; or I am right, and it's they who are the idiots. In either event, this means that between myself and them (that is, our musical leaders: Hubay, etc.) there can be no discussion of music, still less any joint action. [...]

Therefore I have resigned myself to write for my writing-desk only.

So far as appearances abroad are concerned, all my efforts during the last 8 years have proved to be in vain. I got tired of it, and a year ago I stopped pressing for that, too.

If they want to perform something somewhere, they can take my published works and perform them without me; if they ask for a manuscript with some definite intention, I'll give it with pleasure. But I shall never take any steps myself; I've had enough of that during the last 8 years.

My public appearances are confined to *one sole field:* I will do anything to further my research work in musical folklore! I have to be personally active in this field, for nothing can be achieved in any other way; while neither recognition nor public appearances are required for composing."

In the summer of 1912, Bartók went to Norway with his wife via Germany and Sweden.
"…Norwegian peasants—so help me God that I saw in the fields girls gathering hay in dresses that are worn with us, what shall I say, by e.g. simpler school-teachers. Young ladies working in the fields, all of them. Isn't it awful? Here the folk-song is dead—dead for good."

(Bartók to Ion Buşiţia on August 4, 1912)

DAS LEBEN
EIN TRAUM
(913, febr.)

ENMA

117 Bartók and Kodály playing four-hands, February 1913

(Drawing by Mrs. Kodály)

118–120 With his wife and three-year-old son Béla in the
garden of his Rákoskeresztúr home, 1913

(Photos by Zoltán Kodály)

121 At home: September 1915

The year of the Rumanian compositions (*Sonatina, Rumanian Folk Dances* for piano, *Rumanian Christmas Carols, Two Rumanian Folk-Songs* for women's chorus and *Nine Rumanian Songs* for voice and piano).

122 THE COMPOSER'S WIFE AND MOTHER, SEPTEMBER 1915

123 ONE OF THE 1915 RUMANIAN COMPOSITIONS

Title-page of the *Sonatina*, in which folk-tunes are combined with classic principles of form.

126 WITH THE SMALL CELLULOID ANIMALS THE KODÁLYS HAD GIVEN TO LITTLE BÉLA, 1916

Bartók, Mihály Kovács, Mrs. Kodály, little Béla and Mrs. Bartók.

(Photo by Zoltán Kodály)

127 "ON SAFARI" IN THE GARDEN OF THE RÁKOSKERESZTÚR HOUSE, SUMMER 1916

Two naked "aborigines": Béla Bartók Jr. and his playmate, Mihály Kovács.

99

128–129 DURING HIS LAST YEAR OF COMPLETE SECLUSION FROM PUBLIC LIFE, 1916

Four seemingly uneventful years had passed; between February 1913 and January 1917 not a single new work of his had been performed; the World War had even paralysed his activities as a folk-music collector...

...but these seemingly uneventful years were all the more lively and fruitful for Bartók the composer: between 1912 and 1917 he wrote *Four Orchestral Pieces* (op. 12, 1912); the five Rumanian compositions, partly for piano, partly for women's chorus or for voice and piano (1915); the ballet *The Wooden Prince* (op. 13, 1914–16); two cycles of songs (op. 15 and 16, 1915–16); the *Suite* for piano (op. 14, 1916); *Eight Hungarian Folk-Songs* (1907–1917); the *String Quartet No. 2* (op. 17, 1915–17); two series of *Slovak Folk-Songs* for men's chorus and for mixed chorus with piano accompaniment (1917); and the *Fifteen Hungarian Peasant Songs* for piano (1914–17).

130 A PAGE OF THE MANUSCRIPT OF "THE WOODEN PRINCE" (OP. 13)

(Copyright by Universal Edition A. G. Wien)

131 WITH HIS SON DURING A PAUSE IN HIS CREATIVE WORK, 1916

132 THE BUDAPEST OPERA HOUSE WHERE BARTÓK'S FIRST TWO WORKS FOR THE STAGE HAD THEIR WORLD PREMIÈRE

133 "MA", FEBRUARY 1, 1917

Lajos Kassák and Béla Uitz's progressive literature and fine arts periodical was the first to bring out a Bartók issue. It was here that the slow movement of Bartók's *Suite* for piano (op. 14) first appeared in print, along with Kassák's poem dedicated to him, Róbert Berény's 1913 portrait, and Miklós Náray's paper on Bartók.

134 Playbill of the world première of "The Wooden Prince", Bartók's first work for the stage, May 12, 1917

Béla Balázs directed the world première.

"At that time the Opera House had seven conductors, but all of them refused to conduct such a 'concoction'. Finally, a respected Italian guest conductor, Egisto Tango, undertook the task. The Opera House had two stage directors. In the name of the dignity of the Opera House both of them refused point blank to direct such an 'outrage against art'...

"Thus I went to the Intendant and said to him: 'Your Excellency, I have never in my life been on the stage. Entrust me with the production of the ballet. I have never heard how dances are to be coached. Entrust me with the directing and coaching of the corps de ballet, or else The Wooden Prince will never be produced on the stage...

"I do not think that another Intendant, unless he had been a Hungarian Count, would have been willing to embark upon this perilous adventure. But by then Bánffy had become absorbed in designing the sets.

"I worked for two months. I lost fifteen kilos. We launched the attack with Brada, Nirschy, Pallay and the whole fanatic corps de ballet...

"Tickets sold at a high premium. People were prepared for the most uproarious scandal in the history of the Opera House. The reviews had already been written in the spirit and style of 'Little Béla don't compose'.

"It was a memorable night. After the last bars there was a deadly silence in the audience lasting for several seconds. There was not one sound of a handclap. But no whistling nor booing either. It was as if an invisible scale of gigantic proportions was being tipped first one way then the other. In the deadly hush of the auditorium a silent battle, like some internal struggle, was being fought out.

"Then the applause broke out in the galleries and like an avalanche swept down to the boxes and the stalls, carrying before it all the rabble of the press. Many reviews had to be rewritten that night. That was Béla Bartók's first tremendous success."

(From Béla Balázs's reminiscences)

135 THE SET AT THE WORLD PREMIÈRE OF "THE WOODEN PRINCE"

was designed by Count Miklós Bánffy (1874–1950), Intendant of the Opera House at that
time.

136 Róbert Berény's portrait of Béla Bartók

137 THE PRINCE

138 THE FAIRY

Count Miklós Bánffy's sketches for *The Wooden Prince*

139 THE PRINCESS

140 THE WOODEN PUPPET

109

141 Egisto Tango (1873–1951), the Italian conductor of the Budapest Opera House between 1912 and 1919

His name is associated with the world première of both of Bartók's first two stage compositions and it was to him that Bartók dedicated *The Wooden Prince*.

(Painting by Ödön Márffy)

"The year 1917 brought a change in the attitude of the Budapest public towards my compositions. I had the wonderful luck to hear a major work of mine, a musical play with the title *The Wooden Prince*, performed in a perfect manner under the direction of Maestro Egisto Tango."

(From Bartók's Autobiography)

142 The set for the first performance of "Bluebeards's Castle"

Kezdete 7 órakor.

Magy. Kir. 🏛 Operaház.

Pénteken, 1918. május hó 24-én
(bérletszünet 197. szám)

I.

először:

A KÉKSZAKÁLLU HERCEG VÁRA

Opera egy felvonásban. Szövegét irta: Balázs Béla, zenéjét szerzette: Bartók Béla.
Az előadást vezényli Tango Egisto, rendezi Zádor Dezső.

A kékszakállu	✓Kálmán Oszkár	A regős ... ✓Palló Imre
Judit	✓Haselbeck Olga	

30 perc szünet.

II.

A FÁBÓL FARAGOTT KIRÁLYFI

Táncjáték egy felvonásban. Szövegét irta Balázs Béla, zenéjét irta Bartók Béla. — Rendezte Balázs Béla.
Koreografiáját készitette Zöblsch Ottó. Az előadást vezényli Tango Egisto.

Táncolnak:

A királyfi	✓Pallai Anna	Az erdő	
A királykisasszony	Nirschy Emilia	A patak	a teljes tánckar
A tündér	Harmat Boriska	A három virág	
A fabáb	✓Brada Ede		

Kezdete 7 órakor, vége 9¹/₂ órakor.

Az előadás és a felvonások megkezdése után a nézőtérre vezető ajtók zárva maradnak.

A „Magyar Szinpad" a jegyszedőknél 40 fillérért kapható.

MŰSOR:

Szombaton, május 25-én: **A kékszakállu herceg vára** (másodszor). **Bajazzók** (Burián Károly kamaraénekes fellépésével) Kezdete 7 ó.
Vasárnap, 26-án: **Daliás idők muzsikája** (Jótékonycélu előadás) ... Kezdete 7¹/₂ ó.
Hétfőn, 27-én: **Tannhäuser** (Burian Károly kamaraénekes fellépésével) ... Kezdete 6¹/₂ ó.

HELYÁRAK:

HELYEK	Première napi ár	Première előv. ár	Rendes napi ár	Rendes elöv.ár	HELYEK	Première napi ár	Première elöv. ár	Rendes napi ár	Rendes elöv.ár
	K f.	K f.	K f.	K f.		K f.	K f.	K f.	K f.
Páholy: földszinti	88 —	90 —	68 —	70 —	Támlásszék a XVIII—XXIII. sorban	9 20	10 20	8 20	9 20
„ I. emeleti	88 —	90 —	68 —	70 —	II. em. páholyülés az I. sorban	10 20	11 20	9 20	10 20
„ II. „ II. szám	88 —	90 —	68 —	70 —	„ „ a II.	9 20	10 20	8 20	9 20
„ II. „ 2—5.	58 —	60 —	46 —	48 —	III. em. erkélyszék az I.	7 60	8 10	6 60	7 10
Zsöllye	24 20	25 20	19 20	20 20	„ „ a II—V. sorban	6 10	6 60	5 60	6 10
Támlásszék az I—II. sorban	19 20	20 20	15 20	16 20	„ „ a VI—IX.	5 10	5 60	4 60	5 10
„ a III—VI.	17 20	18 20	13 20	14 20	III. em. zártszék az I. sorbcn	3 90	4 20	3 60	3 90
„ a VII—IX.	15 20	16 20	12 20	13 20	„ „ a II.	2 90	3 20	2 60	2 90
„ a X—XIII.	13 20	14 20	11 20	12 20	„ „ a III—IV. sorban	2 40	2 70	2 10	2 40
„ a XIV—XVII. sorban	10 20	11 20	9 20	10 20					

Jegyek válthatók: a napi és a vasárnapi előadásokra a Hajós-utcai pénztárnál, a műsoron hirdetett más előadásokra a Dalszinház-utcai pénztárnál naponként délelőtt 9-1-ig és délután 3—5 óráig (Telefon: 22—49.); ezenkivül egész napon át a következő elárusitó helyeken: 1. Bárd Ferenc és Testvére zeneműkereskedése: Kossuth Lajos-utca 4. szám (Standard palota. Telefon 6—56. és 57—28.) és Andrássy-ut 1. szám. (Telefon 25—13. és 57—08. szám.) 2. Rózsavölgyi és Társa zeneműkereskedése: Szervita-tér 5. (Telefon 10—08.) és Andrássy-ut 45. (Telefon 148—82.)

Esti pénztárnyitás a szinházban 6¹/₂ órakor.

Nyomatott a «Globus» Pénzint. mükintézete és kiadóvállalat r.-t. Budapest. Aradi-utca 8. szám. Telefon 23—48.

143 PLAYBILL OF THE WORLD PREMIÈRE OF "BLUEBEARD'S CASTLE", MAY 24, 1918

144 "I give you another key now. . ."

145 "Blood is oozing through your flowers. . ."

Olga Haselbeck and Oszkár Kálmán, the first to take the roles of Judith and Bluebeard in Bartók's opera.

146 Olga Haselbeck and Oszkár Kálmán with stage director Dezső Zádor and the composer. May 24, 1918

147 During the year of the première of "Bluebeard's Castle", an excursion to Biharfüred with his Rumanian friend Bușiția (left) and Kodály, 1918

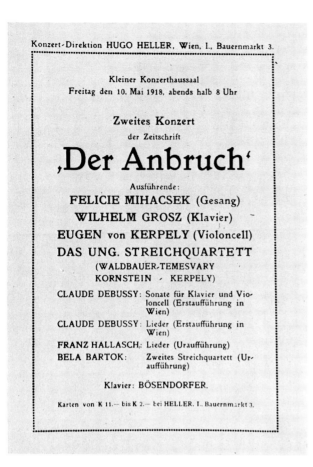

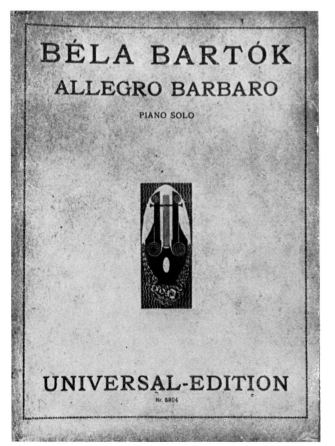

148 THE VIENNA PREMIÈRE OF THE "STRING QUARTET NO. 2"

The programme incorrectly claims that this was the world première; actually that had taken place on March 3, 1918 in Budapest.

149 THE NEW YORK PREMIÈRE OF "TWO PICTURES" (OP. 10)

The work was conducted by Edgar Varèse, the renowned master of experimental twentieth-century music. This was the first orchestral composition of Bartók's to be played in America.

150 TITLE-PAGE OF THE FIRST EDITION OF "ALLEGRO BARBARO" (1918)

"...the greatest success of this year... is that I have succeeded in making an agreement for a longer period with a first-class publishing house. Universal Edition (Vienna) conveyed an acceptable proposition to me already in January... Anyhow, this contract is the greatest success I have scored as a composer up to now."

(To Buşiţia, June 6, 1918)

From 1920 to 1922 the Bartóks lived in the house of József Lukács, father of philosopher Georg Lukács.
"Béla was very proud; he liked to help people but did not accept from others anything he could not return. Finally my father had a very good idea. He asked Béla to do him a very great favour... Father put his request in the form of pretending that he was afraid rooms would be billeted in the house and if Béla and his family moved in this would solve the housing problem of all of us. And so it was. Béla and his family occupied my father's apartment in a house on Gellért Hill, a building which completely disappeared since during the siege of Budapest."

(From the reminiscences of Mrs. Mici Popper, née Lukács)

151 2 GYOPÁR STREET, BUDAPEST, I

152 LETTER TO THE EDITOR-IN-CHIEF OF "SZÓZAT"

During the months of the Hungarian Republic of Councils (1919) Bartók—along with Kodály and Dohnányi—was a member of the Musical Council, which operated under the leadership of Béla Reinitz. After the fall of the Republic of Councils he repeatedly took up the cause of his friend Kodály who was persecuted for his reform endeavours. On February 20, 1920, he wrote to the editor-in-chief of the counter-revolutionary daily *Szózat:* "...nor would I wish to be a member of any musical council from which the greatest musicians of the country are excluded."

153 THE BARTÓK NUMBER OF "MUSIKBLÄTTER DES ANBRUCH"

In March 1921 this Vienna periodical of modern music honoured the forty-year-old composer with a Bartók number.

Describing conditions in the Hungary of 1920 as "pretty bleak", and aware of the continually growing attention his activity as composer, pianist and scholar was receiving abroad, Bartók gave some consideration to the possibility of emigrating. He finally decided, however, to remain in his native land.

154 On a concert tour in Transylvania, February 1922

A picture postcard sent to his mother from Marosvásárhely (now Tîrgu-Mureş, Rumania), where he gave a recital.

155 Piano interlude in the fifth of the "Eight Hungarian Folk-Songs"

Bartók copied these bars for the singer who performed at the 1922 concert in Kolozsvár (now Cluj, Rumania).

156 At the time of the Kolozsvár recital, February 1922

(Photo by Lajos Bátyi)

157 4 Szilágyi Dezső Square, Budapest

Bartók lived here from May 1922 to June 1928. To the right of the taller building may be seen the three front-room windows of his mezzanine flat.

(Photo by Gyula Kertész)

158 IN SALZBURG WITH THE PARTICIPANTS IN THE FESTIVAL OF MODERN CHAMBER MUSIC AT WHICH BARTÓK'S "SONATA No. 1" FOR VIOLIN AND PIANO WAS PERFORMED IN AUGUST, 1922

At the same time the International Society for Contemporary Music (ISCM) was founded on the initiative of English musicologist Edward J. Dent.
From left to right: Rudolf Ganz, Paul Stefan, Frau Heller, Bartók, ?, Carl Friedberg.

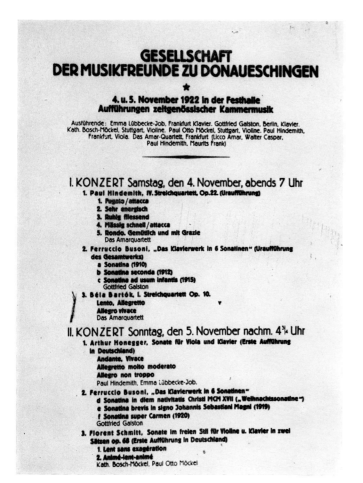

159 DONAUESCHINGEN, NOVEMBER 4, 1922

In the musical life of Europe, slowly recovering from the ravages of the First World War, Bartók's works were ever more frequently performed. At Donaueschingen the Amar Quartet—with Paul Hindemith as the viola-player—performed Bartók's *String Quartet No. 1* (the correct number of the opus being 7).

160 A cubist caricature of the composer of the two "Sonatas" for violin and piano

(Drawing by Béla Sipos)

161 BERLIN, FEBRUARY 9, 1923

A *Melos* Concert with Bartók, Waldbauer and the Waldbauer–Kerpoly String Quartet performing. It was also here that two days earlier, on February 7, the world première of Bartók's *Sonata No. 2* for violin and piano, performed by Waldbauer and he composer, took place.

162–163 HELLERAU, JULY 1923

Bartók's ballet *The Wooden Prince* was performed by the ensemble of the "Dalcroze School" at Hellerau near Dresden. The school director Ernst Ferand-Freund was a musicologist of Hungarian origin. The orchestra was conducted by Eugen Szenkár who three years later conducted the controversial première of Bartók's *Miraculous Mandarin*.

164 Bartók about 1920

165 THE "DANCE SUITE", BARTÓK'S MOST SIGNIFICANT COMPOSITION IN 1923, MARKED THE BEGINNING OF A NEW PHASE IN HIS STYLE OF ORCHESTRATION

(Copyright by Universal Edition A. G. Wien)

167 ERNST VON DOHNÁNYI (1877–1960), WORLD FAMOUS HUN-
GARIAN PIANIST, FOR SEVERAL DECADES THE PRESIDENT-CONDUCTOR
OF THE BUDAPEST PHILHARMONIC SOCIETY AND THE IDOL OF BAR-
TÓK'S YOUTH, HE WAS CONNECTED WITH THE PREMIÈRES OF MANY
OF BARTÓK'S ORCHESTRAL COMPOSITIONS

(Photo by Pál M. Vajda)

November 19, 1923, was a memorable day in the history of
modern Hungarian music. In celebration of the fiftieth
anniversary of the formation of Budapest from the twin
cities of Pest and Buda, the Budapest Philharmonic Society
conducted by Ernst von Dohnányi, presented Dohnányi's
Festival Overture, Kodály's *Psalmus Hungaricus* and Bartók's *Dance Suite*.

125

168 1923 BROUGHT A CHANGE IN BARTÓK'S FAMILY LIFE: HE DIVORCED HIS FIRST WIFE AND MARRIED HIS PUPIL, PIANIST DITTA PÁSZTORY

169 ON A TRIP TO SWITZERLAND

Bartók stands on the extreme left in the middle row; Mrs. Ditta Bartók-Pásztory is seated in the front row, right.

170 Concert of works by Scarlatti–Bach–Bartók in Geneva, December 20, 1923

The two violinists performing at the concert were Jelly d'Arányi and Adila Fachiri-Arányi. Bartók dedicated his two *Sonatas* for violin and piano to Jelly d'Arányi.

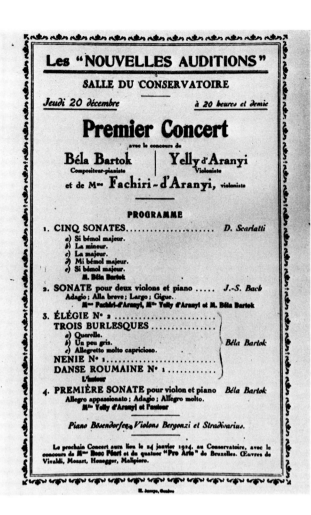

Les "NOUVELLES AUDITIONS"
SALLE DU CONSERVATOIRE
Jeudi 20 décembre   à 20 heures et demie

Premier Concert
avec le concours de
Béla Bartok | Yelly d'Aranyi
Compositeur-pianiste | Violoniste
et de Mme Fachiri-d'Aranyi, violoniste

PROGRAMME

1. CINQ SONATES.................... D. Scarlatti
      a) Si bémol majeur.
      b) La mineur.
      c) La majeur.
      d) Mi bémol majeur.
      e) Si bémol majeur.
         M. Béla Bartok

2. SONATE pour deux violons et piano ..... J.-S. Bach
      Adagio ; Alla breve ; Largo ; Gigue.
         Mme Fachiri-d'Aranyi, Mlle Yelly d'Aranyi et M. Béla Bartok

3. ÉLÉGIE N° 2 ....
   TROIS BURLESQUES ....
      a) Querelle.
      b) Un peu gris.   Béla Bartok
      c) Allegretto molto capricioso.
   NENIE N° 1 ....
   DANSE ROUMAINE N° 1 ....
         L'auteur

4. PREMIÈRE SONATE pour violon et piano   Béla Bartok
      Allegro appassionato ; Adagio ; Allegro molto.
         Mlle Yelly d'Aranyi et l'auteur

Piano Bösendorfer, Violons Bergonzi et Stradivarius.

Le prochain Concert aura lieu le 24 janvier 1924, au Conservatoire, avec le concours de Mme Bace Féari et du quatuor "Pro Arte" de Bruxelles. Œuvres de Vivaldi, Mozart, Honegger, Malipiero.

R. Jarayz, Genève

171 A Bartók concert in Budapest during the inflationary period, November 6, 1923

"Tickets from 1,000–10,000 Crowns"—the poster reveals the rapidly deteriorating economic situation in Hungary. The programme included compositions by Debussy, Scarlatti, Bartók and Kodály.

ZENEMŰVÉSZETI FŐISKOLA   Kedden, november 6-án este fél 9 órakor

Bartók Béla
ZONGORAESTJE

Jegyek **1000-10000** K-ig vigalmi és forgalmi adóval együtt **FODOR HANGVERSENYIRODÁBAN** IV. Váczi-utca 1 (könyvkereskedés) Telefon: **88-61** kaphatók.

172 1923   *(Photo by Strelisky)*

173 1924   *(Photo by Irén Werner)*

174 1924   *(Photo by Erzsi Magyar)*

175 WITH HIS MOTHER,
SEPTEMBER 1925

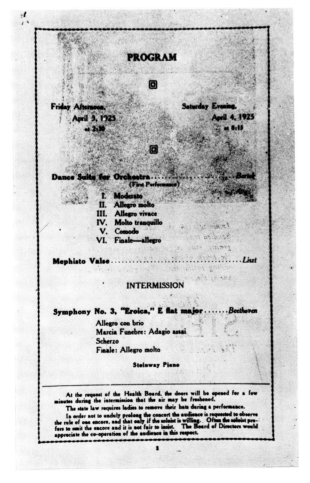

Fritz Reiner conducted The Cincinnati Symphony Orchestra in the American première of *Dance Suite*. From 1923 Fritz Reiner presented Bartók's works, one after the other, to American audiences: the *Suite No. 1* in 1923, the *Suite No. 2* in 1924, *Dance Suite* in 1925, *The Miraculous Mandarin Suite* in 1926, and the *Concerto No. 1* for piano and orchestra in 1928. He played an important part in Bartók's life as well as during the composer's last years in America.

Violinist Zoltán Székely was often his partner in sonata recitals during the twenties and thirties. Bartók dedicated his *Rhapsody No. 2* for violin and piano to him and later composed the *Second Violin Concerto* for him.

(Photo by Mrs. Zoltán Székely)

180 Manuscript of the piano arrangement of "The Miraculous Mandarin" (1918–19, orchestrated in 1924)

(Copyright by Universal Edition A. G. Wien)

132

181 MELCHIOR LENGYEL, DRAMATIST (B. 1880). AUTHOR OF THE LIBRETTO OF "THE MIRACULOUS MANDARIN"

182 PROGRAMME OF THE WORLD PREMIÈRE OF "THE MIRACULOUS MANDARIN". COLOGNE, NOVEMBER 27, 1926

The première—conducted by Eugen Szenkár—scandalized the clergy and the municipal officials of Cologne. On the orders of Konrad Adenauer, then Mayor of Cologne, the mime-play was struck off the programme after the première.

SAMSTAG, DEN 27. NOVEMBER 1926,
ABENDS 7½ UHR
4. OPER MIETREIHE KIII.

Herzog Blaubarts Burg
Oper in einem Akt von Béla Bartók.
Deutsche Übertragung von Wilhelm Ziegler.

Musikalische Leitung: Generalmusikdirektor Eugen Szenkar.
Spielleitung: Generalintendant Hofrat Fritz Remond.

PERSONEN:

Herzog Blaubart . . . . Emil Treskow
Judith . . . . Henny Trundt
Die früheren Frauen . . . . {. Lotte Torger
. Else Hillebrand
. Lilly Büttner

Hierauf:

URAUFFÜHRUNG

Der wunderbare Mandarin
Pantomime in einem Akt von Melchior Lengyel.
Musik von Béla Bartók.

Musikalische Leitung: Generalmusikdirektor Eugen Szenkar.
Spielleitung: Oberregisseur Hans Strohbach.

PERSONEN:

Die drei Strolche . . . . {. Josef Horn
. Hans Salomon
. Josef Weiser
Das Mädchen . . . . Wilma Aug
Der alte Kavalier . . . . Hans Robert
Der Jüngling . . . . Helmut Zehnpfenning
Der Mandarin . . . . Gustav Zeiller

Die Dekorationen und Kostüme für den »wunderbaren Mandarin« sind nach Entwürfen von Hans Strohbach in den Werkstätten der Verein. Stadttheater angefertigt.

Umbesetzungen"infolge von Erkrankungen vorbehalten.

PAUSE NACH »HERZOG BLAUBARTS BURG«

ENDE 9½ UHR

183 Berlin, 1926

Valerie Wolffensteins's drawing, which appeared in the Berlin daily *B. Z. am Mittag*.

Konzert-Direktion ROBERT SACHS, Inhaber E. SACHS und E. KULA

Bernburger Str. 22 PHILHARMONIE Bernburger Str. 22

Montag, den 18. Januar 1926, abends 7¹/₂ Uhr

III. BRUNO WALTER

Konzert mit dem Philharmonischen Orchester

Solist: Béla Bartók

1. Symphonie Nr. IX, C-moll . . . . Haydn
   Allegro
   Andante cantabile
   Menuetto
   Finale. Vivace

2. Rhapsodie für Klavier und Orchester op. 1 Béla Bartók

3. Symphonie Nr. VII, A-dur, op. 92 . . . . Beethoven
   Poco sostenuto — Vivace
   Allegretto
   Presto
   Allegro con brio

Konzertflügel: IBACH

Aus dem Ibach-Hause, Berlin, Steglitzer Str. 27 — Potsdamer Str. 29

IV. BRUNO WALTER

Konzert mit dem Philharmonischen Orchester

Mozart: Requiem

PHILHARMONIE: Montag, den 8. Februar 1926, abends 7¹/₂ Uhr
Oeffentliche Hauptprobe: Sonntag, den 7. Februar 1926, vormittags 11¹/₂ Uhr
Kittel'scher Chor, Lotte Leonard, Fritz Krauss etc.

184 "Bruno Walter Konzert"

January 18, 1926, was the only occasion on which Bartók and Bruno Walter appeared together on the concert platform. Bartók played the solo of his *Rhapsody* for piano and orchestra.

134

185 With his younger son, Péter, then two years old. Szőllőspuszta, 1926

186 With his wife, his son Péter and his sister Elza. Szőllőspuszta, 1926

187 From the Manuscript of the "Sonata" for piano

(Copyright by Universal Edition A. G. Wien)

During 1926 Bartók again devoted himself to piano music: in addition to the *Sonata* he wrote the cycles *Out of Doors* and *Nine Little Pieces* for piano as well as his *Concerto No. 1* for piano and orchestra and some of the *Mikrokosmos* pieces.

188 IN HIS CLASS-ROOM AT THE ACADEMY OF MUSIC IN BUDAPEST, MARCH 1927

(Photo by Alex Kertész)

189 "VILLAGE SCENES"

The *Three Village Scenes*, a cycle of Slovak folk-songs, written for female voices and chamber orchestra in 1926, was first presented to a New York audience by Serge Koussevitzky on November 27, 1927.

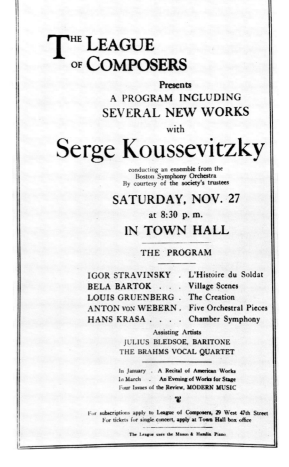

THE LEAGUE OF COMPOSERS

Presents
A PROGRAM INCLUDING
SEVERAL NEW WORKS
with

Serge Koussevitzky

conducting an ensemble from the
Boston Symphony Orchestra
By courtesy of the society's trustees

SATURDAY, NOV. 27
at 8:30 p. m.

IN TOWN HALL

THE PROGRAM

IGOR STRAVINSKY . L'Histoire du Soldat
BELA BARTOK . . . Village Scenes
LOUIS GRUENBERG . The Creation
ANTON VON WEBERN . Five Orchestral Pieces
HANS KRASA . . . . Chamber Symphony

Assisting Artists
JULIUS BLEDSOE, BARITONE
THE BRAHMS VOCAL QUARTET

In January . A Recital of American Works
In March . An Evening of Works for Stage
Four Issues of the Review, MODERN MUSIC

For subscriptions apply to League of Composers, 29 West 47th Street
For tickets for single concert, apply at Town Hall box office

The League uses the Mason & Hamlin Piano

Fifteen years later it was at the suggestion of Koussevitzky that Bartók composed his *Concerto for Orchestra*.

137

190 WITH JOSEPH SZIGETI DURING A REHEARSAL IN THE CONCERT HALL OF THE BUDAPEST ACADEMY OF MUSIC, APRIL 1927

(Drawing by Jenő Feiks)

To Szigeti, his partner in a number of sonata recitals, Bartók later dedicated his *Rhapsody No. 1* for violin and piano, as well as *Contrasts* for violin, clarinet and piano.

191 WITH SZIGETI IN DAVOS, AUGUST 1927

192 ON BOARD THE S.S. "COLUMBIA" SAILING TO AMERICA, DECEMBER 12, 1927

Bartók crossed the Atlantic for the first time in 1927. His concert tour in the United States lasted two and a half months.

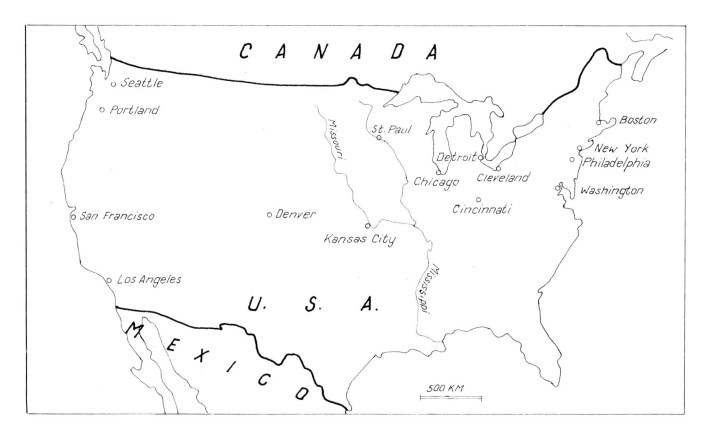

193 Towns Bartók visited in America during his 1927–1928 tour

194 IN NEW YORK, 1927

(Photo by N. Muray)

195 FROM THE PRINTED PROGRAMME OF THE CONCERT IN WHICH BARTÓK MADE HIS AMERICAN DEBUT, DECEMBER 22, 1927

As conductor Willem Mengelberg could not learn the *Piano Concerto No. 1*, Bartók's *Rhapsody No. 1* for piano and orchestra was performed instead at this Carnegie Hall concert in New York.

196 Bartók as seen by a New York photographer...

(Photo by N. Muray)

197 ...and by a New York cartoonist

(Drawing by Aline Fruhaup)

142

198–199 Travelling again ... back to Europe
On board the S.S. "George Washington", March 6, 1928

1. A Polish pianist (I don't know his name)
2. A Hungarian musician (" " " ")
3. Monsieur Robert Schmitz
4. " " " 's daughter, Mlle. Monique
5. The wife of a French-Canadian (writer or actor?) who took this photo
6. Madame Robert Schmitz
7. Il Signor Mario Corti
8. Señor Pablo Casals

A George Washington fedélzetén
1928. márc. 6. án:

1. Egy lengyel zongoraművész (nevét nem tudom
2. Egy magyar zenész (" " ")
3. Monsieur Robert Schmitz
4. " " " lánya, Mlle Monique
5. Egy kanadai francia (író v. miner?) felesége, aré arki fotografiált
6. Madame Robert Schmitz
7. Il Signor Mario Corti
8. Señor Pablo Casals.

200 Poster announcing Bartók's piano recital in Kharkov with compositions of his own and of Kodály's on the programme, January 6, 1929

Early in 1929 Bartók set out on a four-week concert tour in the Soviet Union: he gave recitals in Kharkov, Odessa, Leningrad and Moscow. In the Hungarian musical journal *Zenei Szemle* (Musical Review) he published an interesting report of his experiences and "discoveries".

144

201 In the Soviet Union, January 1929

202 10 Kavics Street, Budapest, III

From 1929 to 1932 the composer lived on the ground floor of this villa. His study is marked by the barred window.

(Photo by Gyula Kertész)

203–205 A winter stroll in Buda with his son Péter, 1929

147

206 Mária Basilides (1886–1946), a famous contralto of Bartók's time

Her enthusiasm for Bartók's and Kodály's music was such that she devoted herself to popularizing their work. She sang at many Bartók concerts. On December 8, 1926, as part of the programme featuring the world première of the *Sonata* for piano she sang Bartók's *Village Scenes* in its original form composed in 1924. This was also a première performance.

207 A Bartók evening in Budapest, March 20, 1929

Performing artists: Mária Basilides, Jenő Kerpely, Imre Waldbauer and the Waldbauer–Kerpely String Quartet.
At this concert the *String Quartet No. 4* and the 'cello and piano version of *Rhapsody No. 1* were presented for the first time in Budapest.

208 Bartók performing at the Vienna concert of the Toldy Circle men's choir of Bratislava

Alban Berg also attended the concert, held on April 25, 1929.
Soon afterwards the Toldy Circle reorganized itself into the "Béla Bartók Choral Society". It was the first group to adopt the composer's name.

Pianist Otto Herz; tenor Ferenc Székelyhidy, soloist for the first performance of *Psalmus Hungaricus;* Bartók; Aladár Tóth, the most eminent music critic of the period; Ernst von Dohnányi; concert manager Imre Bíró; pianist Imre Stefániai.

(Photo by Jenő Antal Molnár)

213 At the Győr railway station after the Liszt–Petőfi concert given by the Sopron Music Society to celebrate its hundredth anniversary

214 In the railway station restaurant, Győr, October 23, 1929

Bartók, an official of the Hungarian Ministry of Culture, Imre Bíró, Otto Herz, Ferenc Székelyhidy, Ernst von Dohnányi, Imre Stefániai.
Bartók sits "alone" in the midst of the group as if separated from the others by an invisible wall.

(Photo by Jenő Antal Molnár)

215 ON THE TRAIN TO BUDAPEST WITH ERNST VON DOHNÁNYI, OCTOBER 23, 1929

(Photo by Jenő Antal Molnár)

216 AT THE BUDAPEST CONGRESS OF THE INTERNATIONAL FEDERATION OF CONCERT MANAGERS, OCTOBER 1929

Seated on the sofa are Gabriella Relle, Bartók, Mme. Failoni and Kodály; Sergio Failoni, conductor of the Budapest Opera House, is seated beside Kodály. Standing (from left to right): first, Imre Bíró; third, Imre Kun, manager of Bartók's concerts from 1934 on; fifth, Otto Herz, who was the piano accompanist at a number of Bartók and Kodály concerts; eighth, Ferenc Székelyhidy.

217 Bartók and his two sons in the garden of the Kavics Street house, 1930

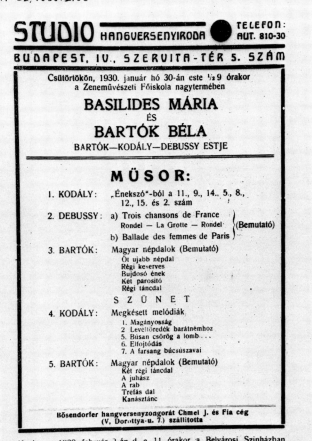

218 A Bartók–Kodály–Debussy concert of Mária Basilides and Bartók held in Budapest on January 30, 1930

Sixteen of the *Twenty Hungarian Folk-Songs* composed in 1929 were first performed at this concert.

220 PROGRAMME OF THE BACH–BARTÓK CONCERT IN BERLIN,
APRIL 3, 1930

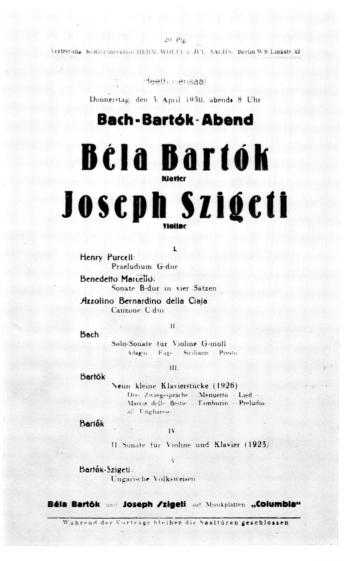

Géza Csorba also did a
statue of Endre Ady,
one of the greatest Hun-
garian poets among Bar-
tók's contemporaries.

(Photo MKF)

Ára: **20** fillér.

1930 ÁPRILIS 22-ÉN, HUSVÉT KEDDJÉN ESTE
½9 ÓRAKOR A ZENEMÜVÉSZETI FÖISKOLA
NAGYTERMÉBEN A STUDIÓ RENDEZÉSÉBEN

A

NYUGAT
ADY-ÜNNEPE

MÜSOR:

1. **MÓRICZ ZSIGMOND:** A költő harca a láthatatlan sárkánnyal.
2. **SIMONYI MÁRIA:** Beszélgetés egy szegfüvel.
   A vállad, a vállad.
   Véresre zúzott homlokkal.
3. **KÁLMÁN OSZKÁR:** Ady—Kodály: Ádám, hol vagy?
   Ady—Kodály: Sirni, sirni, sirni.
4. **FENYŐ MIKSA:** A zseni.
5. **ASCHER OSZKÁR:** Az ős Kaján.
   Nem játszom tovább.
   Levél az apámhoz.

SZÜNET

6. **NAGY ENDRE:** Ady-emlékek.
7. **SCHÖPFLIN ALADÁR:** Ady, a szerelmes-költő.
8. **BABITS MIHÁLY:** Ady.
9. **BASILIDES MÁRIA:** Ady Kodály: Sappho szerelmes éneke.
   Ady—Bartók: Három öszi könnycsepp.
   Ady—Bartók: Nem mehetek hozzád.
   Ady—Bartók: Az ágyam hivogat.
10. **KÜRTI JÓZSEF:** Budapest éjszakája szól.
    Magyar vétkek biborban.

A zongoránál: **BARTÓK BÉLA.**

The periodical *Nyugat* (West) played a major role
in the history of twentieth-century Hungarian
literature. For this evening commemorating poet
Endre Ady the most important figures of Hungarian culture gathered to pay tribute. His poems
set to music by Bartók and Kodály were sung by
Mária Basilides and Oszkár Kálmán, accompanied
by Bartók on the piano.

224 ANTAL DIÓSY'S CARTOON DRAWN ABOUT 1930

"It's too much caricatured," I said touchily...
but Professor Bartók defended Diósy: "Not at
all. It's a very good drawing. I'm just like this."

(Júlia Székely: *Professor Bartók*)

2.

aus dieser 3-fachen (ungar., ruman., slovak.) Quelle entspringt, als eine Verkörperung jener Integrität-Idee betrachten, die heute in Ungarn so sehr betont wird. ... [handwritten letter in German]

"My own idea... is the brotherhood of peoples, brotherhood in spite of all wars and conflicts. I try—to the best of my ability—to serve this idea in my music; therefore I don't reject any influence, be it Slovakian, Rumanian, Arabic or from any other source. The source must only be clean, fresh and healthy!"

(To Octavian Beu, January 10, 1931)

226 "ONLY FROM A CLEAN SOURCE..."

A page of Bartók's pantheistic musical creed, the *Cantata Profana*, whose original Hungarian text he compiled from his own Rumanian *colinda* translations, 1930.

(Copyright by Universal Edition A. G. Wien)

227 The composer of the "Cantata Profana", 1930

(Photo by Dénes Rónai)

Bartók is seated on the left at the corner of the conference table; to his left Karel Čapek and Thomas Mann with Paul Valéry in front of the latter. Bartók had some of the participants sign the back of the photograph.

(Photo by Bacchetta)

228–229 At the Geneva conference of the Comité des Arts et des Lettres de la Coopération Intellectuelle, July 5–8, 1931

230 THE COMPOSER AT THE AGE OF FIFTY WITH HIS
SISTER, MARCH 25, 1931

231 AT HIS PIANO IN HIS HOME ON KAVICS STREET,
NOVEMBER 9, 1931

(Photo by Oszkár Neubauer)

232 "...He was a source of current, an antenna reacting with unprecedented sensitivity and awareness to every vibration in the world and forming in himself the new voice of a changing epoch, of humanity in travail."

(Bence Szabolcsi: "Béla Bartók's Life")

(Photo by Dénes Rónai, 1930)

233 BARTÓK'S PROTEST, IN HIS OWN HAND, AGAINST TOSCANINI'S MALTREATMENT
BY THE ITALIAN FASCISTS AND AGAINST "INTERFERING IN AN AGGRESSIVE MANNER
WITH THE ACTIVITIES OF ARTISTS", MAY 1931

Draft Resolution
1. It is with profound dismay and indignation that the UMZE [New Hungarian Musical Union] learns of the grave insult suffered by A.T. It assures him of its full sympathy and support, and salutes him with the utmost respect and affection.
2. The UMZE notes with anxiety that outside authorities are more and more frequently interfering in an aggressive manner with the activities of artists and no longer shrink back even before the world-wide esteem of a Toscanini. For this reason it considers that the time has come to raise the problem of defence.
It is therefore addressing a circular letter to all sections of the ISCM, asking them to formulate for the Oxford session to be held in July appropriate proposals for the protection of the integrity and autonomy of the arts. It requests the Central Presidium to make preparations for the discussion and to approach other musical—and possibly artistic and literary—organizations, in this matter, so that it will be possible to establish a suitable world organization for the protection of the freedom of the arts.

Béla Bartók

163

234 With Hindemith in Cairo at the time of the congress of Arabian music

From left to right: Gertrud and Paul Hindemith, Jenő Takács, Bartók, March 1932.

235 An excursion in the Sahara, near Cairo

Bartók, Paul and Gertrud Hindemith, E. M. von Hornbostel, Jenő Takács, Curt Schindler, Egon Wellesz.

236 27 (LATER 29) CSALÁN STREET, BUDAPEST, II

The Bartók family lived here from 1932 to 1940; this was the composer's last home in Hungary. The upper-floor room with the open window was his study.

(Photo by Gyula Kertész)

237–240 Four photos taken in the Csalán Street house and its garden, October 1932

The composer grew a moustache while conferred for a time to his rooms by ill health.

The strange patterned cushion preserved the drawings of his son Péter (horse, engine, pianist and even "Daddy-bridge"), designs which Mrs. Bartók embroidered.

241 THE "PIANO CONCERTO No. 2", 1930–1931　　　　*(Copyright by Universal Edition A. G. Wien)*

One of the outstanding compositions of Bartók's "Neo-Baroque" period.
The picture shows the piano part in the "short-hand" used by Bartók when he played the solo himself.

242 WITH THE CONDUCTOR HANS ROSBAUD IN FRANKFURT AM MAIN
BEFORE THE WORLD PREMIÈRE OF THE "PIANO CONCERTO NO. 2" ON
JANUARY 23, 1933

This was Bartók's last public appearance in Germany

243 OTTO KLEMPERER CONDUCTED THE FIRST PERFORMANCE OF THE
"PIANO CONCERTO NO. 2" IN VIENNA ON JUNE 7, 1933

At the time Bartók was annoyed with the audiences of the Hungarian capital and had therefore left the first Budapest performance entirely to Louis Kentner.

169

244–245 A Bartók–Waldbauer sonata recital in Budapest, January 12, 1934

After several years' "voluntary compulsory silence" Bartók made a comeback in the concert hall of the Budapest Academy of Music. In the row of seats in front of the concert platform —leaning back slightly —is seated white-haired Béla Reinitz, a noted song-composer who had been in charge of the Budapest Musical Council in 1919. After the fall of the Hungarian Republic of Councils Reinitz was arrested. Bartók dedicated to him his *Five Songs* op. 16 as an expression of sympathy.

(Photo by Kata Kálmán)

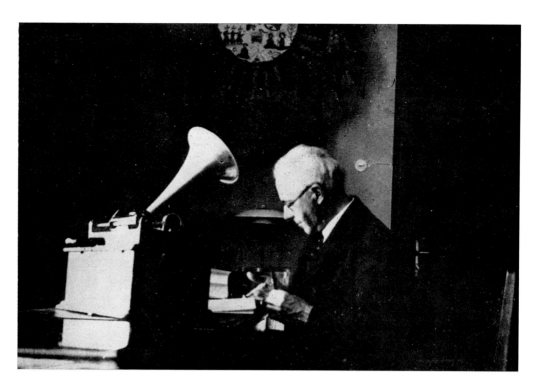

246 BUCHAREST, FEBRUARY 1934

Bartók studying recordings of Rumanian folk music at the Federation of Rumanian Composers.

247 CLASS REUNION

Bartók and his former secondary-school class-mates, 35 years later in Budapest. In the middle, writer Mózes Gaál, their former master, 1934.

(Photo by Gyula Schäffer)

Bartók played his *Piano Concerto No. 2* in the Swedish capital on April 18, 1934, at a concert conducted by Czech conductor Václav Talich.

"In the thirties... Talich and the Prague Philharmonic Orchestra performed the *Dance Suite* in Hungary. Of the performances Bartók said with an impish smile: 'This counterproof has been useful because, on grounds of the Budapest performances, I was on the point of believing that I knew nothing of orchestration; now I can see that I have an inkling of it after all!' "

(Antal Molnár: Bartók's Art)

249 IN STOCKHOLM MUSEUM OF MUSICAL HISTORY WITH TOBIAS NORLIND, APRIL 19, 1934

250–251 Whimsical snapshots of a birthday in Csalán Street. Bartók with his wife, mother, son Péter and sister

252 THE HUNGARIAN ACADEMY OF SCIENCES IN BUDAPEST

At his own request Bartók was relieved of his chair at the Academy of Music in 1934 and was assigned to the Hungarian Academy of Sciences, where he worked preparing the publication of the complete material of Hungarian folk music until his departure in 1940 to America.

253 WITH EARPHONES, REVISING HIS EARLIER NOTES ON FOLK-MUSIC
RECORDING

254 COMPARATIVE MUSIC FOLKLORE

From a 1934 paper by Bartók entitled "Hungarian Folk Music
and the Folk Music of the Neighbouring Peoples", he discusses
the interaction between the folk music of peoples living side
by side. The facsimile shows related Hungarian and Rumanian
folk-songs collected by Bartók and written out in his own hand.

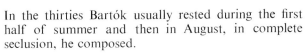

In the thirties Bartók usually rested during the first half of summer and then in August, in complete seclusion, he composed.

178

259–262

Bartók spent most of his summer holidays in Switzerland during the thirties. The photos taken there speak eloquently of his feeling for nature.

Pr.-66. 1935. III 19

Kedden. 1935 március 19.-én este 8 órakor
a Zeneművészeti Főiskola nagytermében a

Waldbauer-Hannover Temesváry-Kerpely

vonósnégyes

ünnepi hangversenye

V. (jubiláris) bérleti est

BARTÓK BÉLA

közreműködésével

Rendezi: „KONCERT" RT. hangversenyvállalat
IV., VÁCI-UCCA 23. SZÁM. Telefon: 88—4—64 és 83 3—09.

MŰSOR ÁRA: 80 FILLÉR

On March 29, 1935, at a gala concert celebrating their twenty-fifth anniversary, the Waldbauer–Kerpely String Quartet re-played the programme of their 1910 concert—the first to consist entirely of Bartók and Kodály works. In addition to the two composers' *First String Quartets*, Kerpely and Bartók played Kodály's *Sonata* for 'cello and piano.

265–266 With his mother and his son Péter in the garden
of the Csalán Street villa, May 1935

267 WITH JOSEPH SZIGETI, BEFORE A BUDAPEST CONCERT, OCTOBER 20, 1935

268 BARTÓK ON SZIGETI

"The life of a musician—however strange this may sound—does not abound in moving and beautiful experiences. To listen to Joseph Szigeti playing the concertos of Brahms, Mendelssohn and Bach is one of the joys of my life. His production is an unforgettable, great experience."

Béla Bartók

269 THE B.B.C. TRANSMITTING A CONCERT FROM DOHNÁNYI'S BUDAPEST HOME

270 IN THE STUDIOS OF RADIO BUDAPEST

271 POWERFUL HANDS, FAR-SEEING, FINE EYES...

In London a few days before his concert at Queen's Hall. January, 1936.

(Photo New York Times, London)

272 ON FRANZ LISZT...

His inaugural lecture at the Hungarian Academy of Sciences. February 3, 1936.

(Photo by Gyula Schäffer)

1897

1899

1899

1903

1914

1919

1934

1934

1938

1944

1945

1945

273 Bartók's signatures

1897–1945

274–275 Bartók's last concert in Vienna on May 18, 1936

The orchestra of the Budapest Philharmonic Society, conducted by Ernst von Dohnányi, played Liszt's *Dance Macabre*, with Bartók at the piano.

ÖSTERREICHISCH-UNGARISCHE GESELLSCHAFT

Montag, den 18. Mai 1936. abends 8 Uhr
Grosser Musikvereinssaal
✳
Erstes Konzert
der
**BUDAPESTER PHILHARMONISCHEN
GESELLSCHAFT**
(ORCHESTER DER K. UNG. OPER)
Dirigent:
Dr. ERNST v. DOHNÁNYI

Solist:
BÉLA BARTÓK
(Klavier)

PROGRAMM:

1. BEETHOVEN: Ouverture zu Göthes Trauerspiel „Egmont"
2. BRAHMS: III. Sinfonie, F-dur
    I. Allegro con brio
    II. Andante con moto
    III. Poco allegretto
    IV. Allegro

PAUSE

3. ZÁDOR: Ungarisches-Capriccio (Erstaufführung)
4 LISZT: Totentanz (Solist *Béla Bartók*)
5. BARTÓK: Der wunderbare Mandarin
    Musik aus der gleichnamigen Pantomime
    (in Wien zum ersten Male)
6 BERLIOZ: Ungarischer Marsch

Bechstein-Flügel von der Firma Josef Saphir, Nestroy Platz 1.

Konzertdirektion: DR. ARTUR HOHENBERG

2

276 WITH THE NEW HUNGARIAN STRING QUARTET, MARCH 1936

Sándor Végh–László Halmos–Dénes Koromzay–Vilmos Palotai–Bartók

(Photo by József Pécsi)

Der ungarische Komponist Béla Bartók.

Zeichnung von Robert Fuchs.

277 ROBERT FUCHS'S DRAWING IN THE MAY 23, 1936 ISSUE OF THE VIENNA DAILY "NEUE FREIE PRESSE"

1. Losonc (Lučenec)
2. Rimaszombat (Rimavska Sobota)
3. Kassa (Košice)
4. Komárom (Komárno)
5. Nyíregyháza
6. Szatmár (Satu Mare)
7. Debrecen
8. Nagyvárad (Oradea)
9. Kecskemét
10. Békéscsaba
11. Belényes (Beiuş)
12. Marosvásárhely (Tg. Mureş)
13. Szeged
14. Makó
15. Nagyszentmiklós (Sînnicolau Mare)
16. Arad
17. Szászsebes (Sebeş)
18. Sepsiszentgyörgy (Sfîntu Gheorghe)

278 Map of Bartók's European concert and lecturing tours

188

After eighteen years, in October 1936, the Budapest Opera House revived Bartók's opera. Gusztáv Oláh's set is shown here.

279 "Bluebeard's Castle"

280 Bartók with the performers in the revival

Beside the composer, Ella Némethy, who sang the part of Judith; beside her the conductor Sergio Failoni; behind them director Kálmán Nádasdy, the production's Bluebeard, Mihály Székely, and set designer Gusztáv Oláh.

189

In Ankara, on the terrace of the Halkevi Palace: (?), Bey Hasan Ferid, Bartók, Bey Halil Bedi, Bey Necil Kâzim, Bey Ulvi Cemal, Bey Ahmed Adnan. *At the bottom:* an itinerant singer.

281 BARTÓK'S LAST FOLK-SONG COLLECTING TOUR—TURKEY, NOVEMBER 1936

282 WITH MEMBERS OF THE NOMADIC KUMARLI TRIBE

283 Sunset on Mount Tüyshüz

284 On the way to visit the nomadic mountain tribes

To Bartók's left, in a grey hat: A. Adnan Saygun (given as Bey Ahmed Adnan in the composer's 1936 notes), professor at the Istanbul Conservatoire, composer and folk-music scholar.

Megállapodás

Bartók Béla .... (lakása): Bpest. II. Csalán utca 27. , *mint szerző*

és a **MAGYAR KÓRUS** lap- és zeneműkiadó k. f. t. Budapest, *mint kiadó között.*

1. *A szerző alábbi műveit átengedi megjelentetésre a kiadónak:* Imult időkből- Tavasz - Ne hagyj itt Jószágigéző - Levél az otthoniakhoz - Játék - Leánynéző - Héjja - Ne menj el - Van egy gyürüm - Senkim a világon - Cipósütés - Huszárnóta - Resteknek nótája - Bolyongás - Leánycsufoló - Legénycsufoló - Ujévi köszöntő - Lánykörő - Keserves e Madárdal - Csujogató - Bánat - Ne láttalak volna - Elment a madárka - Párnás táncdal Kánon - Isten veled!

2. *A kiadó elvállalja a fentnevezett mű(vek) kiadását. Vállalja az előállítás, forgalombahozatal, hirdetés, (árjegyzék), raktározás, kezelés költségeit, ugyszintén a sajtó és tiszteletpéldányok előállításának és végül könyvkereskedők bizományi százalékának terhét.*

3. *Ezzel szemben szerző átenged egyszersmindenkorra minden — a* .... *szerzőjogi törvények szerinti — jogot a kiadónak, beleértve a tetszés szerinti számu előállításnak, a kiadás(ok) időpontjának, a művek eladási árának megállapítási, illetőleg megváltoztatási jogát. Mindennemű elintézés helye Budapest.* Be a jog asenben sak a magyarnyelvü kiadásra szól.

4. *Ugyanigy a kiadó rendelkezik esetleges gépzenei felvételek, filmre vitel, távolbaadítással kapcsolt előadás stb. joga felett. Az ily eljárdsokból eredő jövedelem felerészben a szerzőé, felerészben a kiadóé.*

5. ~~As eredeti kéziratok a kiadó tulajdonába megy át. A kiadónak joga van a mű kéziratában olyan változtatásokat kívánni, melyeket kiadványai egyöntetűsége és a szakszerűség szempontjából szükségesnek tart. (Cim, csálamok megnevezése, a partitúra beosztása stb. stb.)~~

6. ~~Fenti művek zenei témáiból alkotott esetleges uj művét a szerző nem bocsájtja más kiadó rendelkezésére.~~

7. *A kiadónak jogában áll fentnevezett műveket, vagy azoknak egyes részleteit tankönyvekbe, példatárakba és egyéb gyüjteményes művekbe felvenni,* de csakis a szerző előzetes engedélyével.

8. *Külön megállapodás:* Szerzői honorárium az eladott művek bruttó értéke után 25 százalék. Elszámolás minden év juniusában.
   A 4. ponthoz: Az e pontban felsorolt jogok szintén csak a magyarnyelvü felvételekre vonatkoznak.
   Az eladási díjakból a kiadó csak a magyarországi előadások után részesedik.
   Az 5. és 6. pontot töröltük.

Budapest 1936 december 31-én   Budapest 1936 december 31-én

Bartók Béla   MAGYAR KÓ...
           ZENEMŰKIADO

Budapest, 1937. febr. 20. *Bartók Béla*

Urged by Kodály to follow his example, Bartók took part as well in the movement aimed at bringing music to the masses.

"Hungarian children do not know yet what present, abiding for a lifetime, they were given for Christmas 1936"—thus Kodály greeted Bartók's choruses for children.

285 Two and three-part choruses for children and female chorus a cappella

286 AT THE PIANO IN THE STUDY OF HIS CSALÁN STREET HOME, 1936   *(Photo by Kata Kálmán)*

January 21, 1937, was a notable date in the history of twentieth-century music: the Basler Kammerorchester, conducted by Paul Sacher, first performed the work Bartók had composed specially for them: a masterpiece of unbridled fantasy and strict discipline, of the soul's descent to the inferno and of its soaring to infinite heights.

BASLER KAMMERORCHESTER LEITUNG PAUL SACHER

DONNERSTAG 21. JAN. 1937 20.15 UHR ALTER KONZERTSAAL

3. KONZERT

IM ABONNEMENT
(JUBILÄUMSKONZERT ZUR ERINNERUNG AN DAS ERSTE KONZERT DES B.K.O. AM 21. JAN. 1927)

SOLISTEN
FELIX LOEFFEL BASS BERN
ADRIAN AESCHBACHER KLAVIER BERLIN-ZÜRICH

PROGRAMM

CONRAD BECK
geb 1901

RHAPSODIE (CONCERTINO NO. 2) FÜR KLAVIER UND KAMMERORCHESTER*
Maestoso · Allegro · Adagio · Allegro moderato · Molto tranquillo · Allegro molto vivace

WILLY BURKHARD
geb 1900

«DAS EWIGE BRAUSEN» FÜR EINE BASSTIMME UND KAMMERORCHESTER, OP. 46*
Nach Gedichten von Knut Hamsun (deutsch von Hermann Hiltbrunner)

PAUSE

BÉLA BARTÓK
geb 1881

MUSIK FÜR SAITENINSTRUMENTE*
Andante tranquillo · Allegro · Adagio · Allegro molto

* Uraufführung

Konzertmeister Gertrud Flugel   Texte umstehend

Karten zu Fr 6.60, 4.95, 3.30, 2.20 bei Hug & Co, Freiestrasse 70a und an der Abendkasse. Verkauf ab Mittwoch, 13 Januar. Für Mitglieder Preisermassigung und Vorbezugsrecht ab Montag, 11 Januar. Programm mit Text 30 Cts

4. Konzert im Ab., Donnerstag, 4 März, 20.15 Uhr, **Martinskirche**, Rosenmuller Aus den «Lamentationes Jeremiae Prophetae» Ingegneri Motetten, **Malipiero**: «La Passione» Solisten Ginevra Vivante (Sopran), Salvatore Salvati, Max Meili (Tenor) Francesco Rosati (Bass) Adolf Hamm (Orgel)

288 On the Schönenberg, with composer Conrad Beck and conductor Paul Sacher, January 1937

(Photo by Prof. O. Müller)

290 PAUL SACHER'S SCORE, DEDICATED TO HIM BY BARTÓK

It was from this score that Sacher conducted the first performance of the work.

195

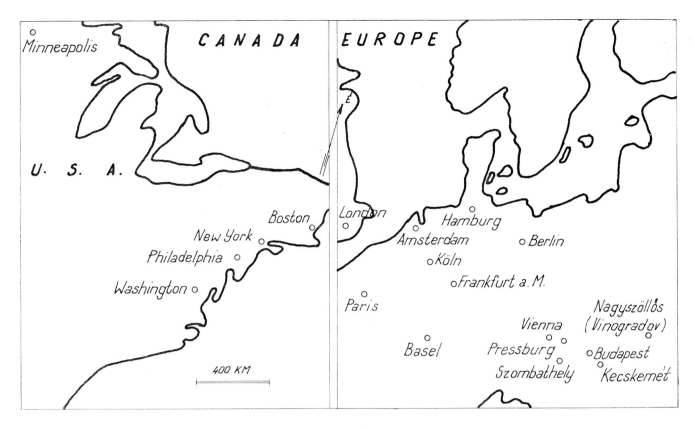

291 Forty world premières of Bartók's works by cities and dates

AMSTERDAM
   Concerto No. 2 for violin and orchestra, March 23, 1939
BASEL
   Music for String Instruments, Percussion and Celesta, January 21, 1937
   Sonata for Two Pianos and Percussion, January 16, 1938
   Divertimento for string orchestra, June 11, 1940
   Concerto No. 1 for violin and orchestra, May 30, 1958
BERLIN
   Sonata No. 2 for violin and piano, February 7, 1923
BOSTON
   Concerto for Orchestra, December 1, 1944
BUDAPEST
   Kossuth, symphonic poem, January 13, 1904
   Suite No. 2 for orchestra, November 22, 1909
   String Quartet No. 1, March 19, 1910
   Two Pictures for orchestra, April 20, 1916
   The Wooden Prince, May 12, 1917
   String Quartet No. 2, March 3, 1918
   Bluebeard's Castle, May 24, 1918
   Four Orchestral Pieces, January 9, 1922
   Dance Suite for orchestra, November 19, 1923
   Sonata for piano, December 8, 1926
   Scherzo for piano and orchestra, September 28, 1961
COLOGNE
   The Miraculous Mandarin, November 27, 1926
   FRANKFURT AM MAIN
   Concerto No. 1, for piano and orchestra, July 1, 1927
   Concerto No. 2, for piano and orchestra, January 23, 1933
HAMBURG
   String Quartet No. 3, February 8, 1929

KECSKEMÉT
   Allegro Barbaro, February 1, 1913
LONDON
   Cantata Profana, May 25, 1934
MINNEAPOLIS
   Concerto for viola and orchestra, December 2, 1949
NAGYSZŐLLŐS
   The Course of the Danube, May 1, 1892
NEW YORK
   Contrasts, January 9, 1939
   String Quartet No. 6, January 20, 1941
   Concerto for two pianos, percussion and orchestra, January 21, 1943
   Sonata for Solo Violin, November 26, 1944
PARIS
   Rhapsody for piano and orchestra, August 8, 1905
PHILADELPHIA
   Concerto No. 3, for piano and orchestra, February 8, 1946
POZSONY
   Rhapsody for piano, September 4, 1906
SZOMBATHELY
   Hungarian Peasant Songs for orchestra, March 18, 1934
VIENNA
   Piano Quintet, November 21, 1904
   Suite No. 1 for orchestra, November 29, 1905
   Fourteen Bagatelles, June 29, 1908
   Sonata No. 1 for violin and piano, February 8, 1922
WASHINGTON
   String Quartet No. 5, April 8, 1935

196

292–297 "Parisian variations, 1937"   *(Photo by Studio Lipnitzky)*

298 Bartók festival of "the singing Great Plain" in Kecskemét

In this small provincial town—Kodály's native town—the world première of twenty-one of Bartók's works was held on April 18, 1937.

Shown with Bartók and concert guests is one of the ensembles which performed at this series of gala concerts: the choir of the Teachers' Training College of the Calvinist Church of Nagykőrös, and their conductor Barna Márton. In the second row writer György Sárközi and music critic Viktor Lányi are standing on the left, and conductor Zoltán Vásárhelyi on the far right; conductor Sergio Failoni is seated left to Bartók, conductor Issay Dobrowen and music critics Aladár Tóth and Alexander Jemnitz to his right.

299 WITH VIOLINIST ANDRÉ GERTLER IN BUDAPEST, FEBRUARY 1937

300 GALA CONCERT AT THE BUDAPEST MUNICIPAL THEATRE

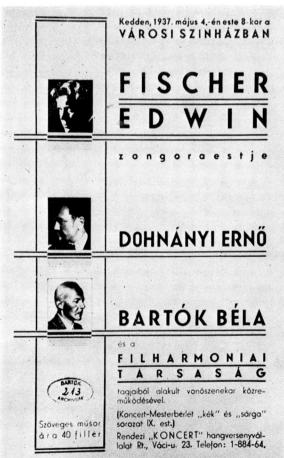

Edwin Fischer, Ernst von Dohnányi and Béla Bartók played Bach's *Concertos* for three pianos in D Minor and C Major, May 4, 1937.

Z. 13

Volume II

BÉLA BARTÓK
Mikrokosmos

153 PROGRESSIVE PIANO PIECES
IN SIX VOLUMES

BOOSEY & HAWKES Inc.

153 Progressive Piano Pieces; a compendium of Bartók's world of music (1926–1937).

First page of Bartók's rough draft.

303 Bartók with his eighty-year-old mother, June 1937

304 Bartók and his wife with Rumanian folk-music scholar Constantin Brăiloiu and Mme. Brăiloiu in the garden of the Csalán Street house, 1937

ZENEMŰVÉSZETI FŐISKOLA

Pénteken, 1938 január hó 7.-én, este 8 órakor

THOMÁN ISTVÁN

75 éves születésnapja alkalmából
rendezett
ünnepi hangverseny

MŰSOR:

1 UNGAR IMRE: *Bach*: a) Praeludium és fuga cis-moll
       „   b)   „   c-moll
       „   c)   „   Cis-dur

2 SZÉKELY ARNOLD: a) *Chopin*: Nocturne cis-moll
                b) *Debussy*: Prelude a-moll

3. BARTÓK BÉLA: *Bartók*: a) I. rondo
                     b) I. sirató ének
                     c) Allegro barbaro

SZÜNET

4. KEÉRI-SZÁNTÓ IMRE: *Chopin*: a) Ballada g-moll
                            b) Nocturne es-moll
                            c) Scherzo b-moll

5. DOHNÁNYI ERNŐ: *Dohnányi*: Négy rapszódia op. 11.
                     Thomán Istvánnak ajánlva

A STEINWAY & SONS hangversenyzongorát a KOHN ALBERT cég
(IV. Bécsi-ucca 3) szállította.

Rendezi: „KONCERT" hangverseny vállalat IV. Váci ucca 23.
Telefon: 188—464 és 183—309
Á R A   30   F I L L É R

On January 7, 1938, Bartók played at a birthday concert held in honour of his former piano professor István Thomán.

306 Cigarette break, January 1938

307 "Sonata for Two Pianos and Percussion"

Commissioned by the Basel department of the International Society for Contemporary Music, this work was composed by Bartók in 1937. It was first performed in Basel on January 16, 1938. The two piano parts were played by Bartók and his wife, Ditta Pásztory, those for percussion by Fritz Schiesser and Philipp Rühlig.

The picture shows Bartók and his wife after the première, in the home of Prof. Oscar Müller and his wife.

(Photo by Prof. O. Müller)

308 The part for percussion lithographed from Bartók's handwriting with corrections in the composer's own hand

(Copyright by Boosey & Hawkes Music Publishers Limited London)

(Photo by Ferenc Bónis)

310 "Be always so fresh and gay"

Bartók's entry into Aya Müller's keepsake album: the opening theme of the third movement of the *Sonata for Two Pianos and Percussion.*

311 With André Gertler in the violinist's Brussels home, 1938

312 In Brussels, 1938

(Photo by Charles Leirens)

Írók, művészek, tudósok deklarációja a magyar társadalomhoz és a törvényhozás tagjaihoz

A felsőház bizottsága módosította a választójogi javaslatot

313 A declaration by writers, artists and scientists addressed to Hungarian society and the members of the legislature protesting against the racial discrimination Law then being drafted. May 5, 1938

"Let every contemporary think over the responsibility he will have to bear if, in spite of the protests of conscience, a law is enacted here, of which, in times to come, every Hungarian will have to think with shame!"—reads the final paragraph of the declaration, which was signed among others by Bartók and Kodály.

The Law was soon enacted all the same.

314 "Let every contemporary think over the responsibility he will have to bear..."

(Photo by Kata Kálmán)

315 THE BARTÓKS WITH ERNEST ANSERMET IN THE OFFICE OF THE BUDAPEST PHILHARMONIC SOCIETY, OCTOBER 31, 1938

(Photo by Gyula Schäffer)

316–317 THE "SONATA FOR TWO PIANOS AND PERCUSSION" WAS FIRST PERFORMED IN HUNGARY ON OCTOBER 31, 1938—MRS. BARTÓK'S BIRTHDAY

The concert was conducted by Ernest Ansermet. To the final rehearsal Bartók invited Aladár Rácz, the famous Hungarian cimbalom artist whom Saint-Saëns had called "the Liszt of the cimbalom".

318 FROM THE SCORE OF THE "VIOLIN CONCERTO"

*(Copyrigt by Boosey & Hawkes Music Publishers
Limited London)*

Bartók had already in his youth written one violin concerto, but this was not published in his lifetime. At the request of Zoltán Székely, he wrote another, the *Violin Concerto* No. 2, which was completed on New Year's Eve 1938, and first performed in March 1939.

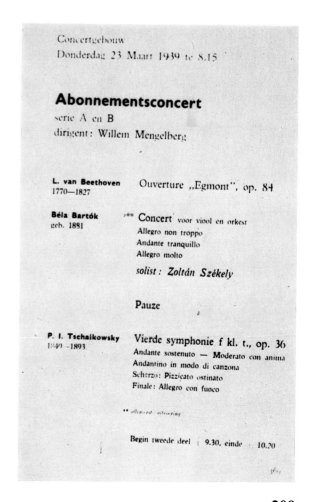

319 PROGRAMME OF THE WORLD PREMIÈRE OF THE "VIOLIN CONCERTO" No. 2

Zoltán Székely was soloist under the baton of Willem Mengelberg, Amsterdam, March 23, 1939.

320 In 1938   *(Photo by Marianne Reismann)*

321 THE FIRST TWO-PIANO RECITAL IN BUDAPEST BY BÉLA BARTÓK AND HIS WIFE, DITTA PÁSZTORY, MARCH 29, 1939

(Photo by Gyula Schäffer)

In the Piazza San Marco with pianist Otto Herz, April 5, 1939.

(Photo by Ede Zathureczky)

323 DURING A CONCERT INTERVAL IN THE BUDAPEST MUNICIPAL THEATRE, MAY 15, 1939

Bartók, conductor Viktor Vaszy, violinist Guila Bustabo and Imre Kun, concert manager.

324–325 In Oberengadin, Switzerland, Summer 1939

Top: The Bartóks and their son Péter, fifteen years of age.
Bottom: the composer, Mme. Müller-Widmann, Aya and Elisabeth Müller, and Valerie Kägi.
Bartók wrote some significant letters to Mme. Müller-Widmann in the thirties.

326 A HAPPY CAREFREE MOMENT—IN THE SHADOW OF IMPENDING WORLD CATASTROPHE, 1939

(Photo by Prof. O. Müller)

327 Châlet Aellen, Saanen

"Somehow I feel like a musician of olden times—the invited guest of a patron of the arts. For here I am, as you know, entirely the guest of the Sachers; they see to everything—from a distance. In a word, I am living alone—in an ethnographic object: a genuine peasant cottage. The furnishings are not in character, but so much the better, because they are the last word in comfort ... Recently, even the weather has been favouring me—this is the 9th day that we've had beautifully clear skies, and not a drop of rain has fallen since the 9th. However, I can't take advantage of the weather to make excursions: I have to work. And for Sacher himself—on a commission (something for a string orchestra); in this respect also my position is like that of the old-time musician. Luckily the work went well, and I finished it in 15 days (a piece of about 25 minutes), I just finished it yesterday."

(Bartók, in a letter to his son Béla, dated August 18, 1939)

These dispassionate words signalled the birth of the *Divertimento* for string orchestra. It was here also that Bartók began composing the *String Quartet No. 6.*

This work, begun in Saanen and completed in Budapest in November 1939, was the last that Bartók
composed in Europe.

**BASLER
KAMMERORCHESTER**
KAMMERCHOR UND KAMMERORCHESTER
LEITUNG PAUL SACHER

20.15 UHR   NEUER CASINO-SAAL
DIENSTAG 11. JUNI 1940

5. KONZERT

PROGRAMM

ERNST KRENEK
geb. 1900

SYMPHONISCHES STÜCK FÜR STREICHORCHESTER,
OP. 86 (1939) *
Andante, molto sostenuto · Allegro, ma non troppo · Adagio ·
Andante sostenuto

Paul Sacher und dem Basler Kammerorchester gewidmet

WILLY BURKHARD
geb. 1900

«GENUG IST NICHT GENUG!» KANTATE NACH GEDICHTEN
VON C. F. MEYER FÜR GEMISCHTEN CHOR MIT BEGLEITUNG
VON STREICHORCHESTER, 2 TROMPETEN UND PAUKEN,
OP. 55 (1938-39) *
I. Fülle (Lebendig)   II. Unter den Sternen (Sehr lebhaft · Langsam)
III. Der römische Brunnen (Ruhig und gemessen)

PAUSE

BELA BARTOK
geb. 1881

DIVERTIMENTO FÜR STREICHORCHESTER (1939) *
I. Allegro non troppo   II. Molto adagio   III. Allegro assai

Paul Sacher und dem Basler Kammerorchester gewidmet

Konzertmeister: Gertrud Flügel   * Uraufführung

Ende ca. 21.45 Uhr   Text umstehend

Karten zu Fr. 6.60, 4.95 und 3.50 bei Hug & Co., Freiestrasse 70a und an der Abendkasse 19.30 Uhr.
Verkauf ab Dienstag, 7. Mai.   Für Mitglieder Preisermässigung und Vorbezugsrecht ab Montag,
6. Mai. Militär an der Abendkasse halbe Preise. Programm mit Text 20 Cts.

329 PROGRAMME OF THE WORLD PREMIÈRE IN BASEL OF THE
"DIVERTIMENTO" FOR STRING ORCHESTRA WHICH WAS WRITTEN
AT SAANEN, JUNE 11, 1940

Late in 1939 Bartók lost his beloved mother and with her the last remaining impediment at home which practically up to the last moment was making it impossible to him to leave Hungary, a country on the brink of war. "That is the imminent danger that Hungary will surrender to this regime of thieves and murderers," Bartók wrote right after the Austrian *Anschluss.* "...and how I can then go on living in such a country or—which means the same thing—working, I simply cannot conceive." In the spring of 1940 Bartók made an exploratory trip to the United States.

330 On board the S.S. "Rex" sailing to America, April 1940

Bartók is seated with his back to the rail in cap and sunglasses; beside him is pianist Béla Böszörményi-Nagy.

331 In the New York home of László Harsányi, pastor of the Calvinist church, May 7, 1940

On Bartók's right, violinist Fery Roth, leader of the Roth Quartet.

332–333 Rehearsal and concert with Szigeti

Their New York recital took place on April 21, 1940.

334–335 "Contrasts" for violin, clarinet and piano

This trio, written for Szigeti and American jazz clarinetist Benny Goodman, was recorded in New York by the Columbia Record Company in April 1940.

After the trip to America in the spring, Bartók returned home for a few months—only to leave again with his wife for a longer stay in the United States.

Kedden, 1940. október hó 8-án este
fél 9 órakor a Zeneművészeti Főiskola
nagytermében

BARTÓK BÉLA

és

PÁSZTORY DITTA

zenekari estje

a SZÉKESFŐVÁROSI ZENEKART

vezényli:

FERENCSIK JÁNOS

Műsoron: Bach: A-dur zongoraverseny
(Bartók), Mozart: F-dur zongoraverseny
(Pásztory), Mozart: Kétzongorás Es-dur
verseny (Bartók-Pásztory), Bartók: Mik-
rokozmosz c. sorozatból (Bartók).

Jegyek 1.50-12 P-ig a Hangversenyrendező kft.
irodájában, VI. Andrássy-ut 26. Telefon: 125-899,
Rózsavölgyinél és a Zeneakadémia portásánál.

337 PROGRAMME OF THE BARTÓKS' LAST CONCERT IN BUDAPEST

The increasing threat of Nazism prompted Bartók to go into voluntary exile. There was no external cause for this: he left because of his conviction. On October 8, 1940, he and his wife gave their last recital in Budapest—and Europe. A few days later they left Hungary.

338–339 THE FAREWELL CONCERT IN BUDAPEST

The Municipal Orchestra conducted by János Ferencsik.

(Photo by Károly Escher)

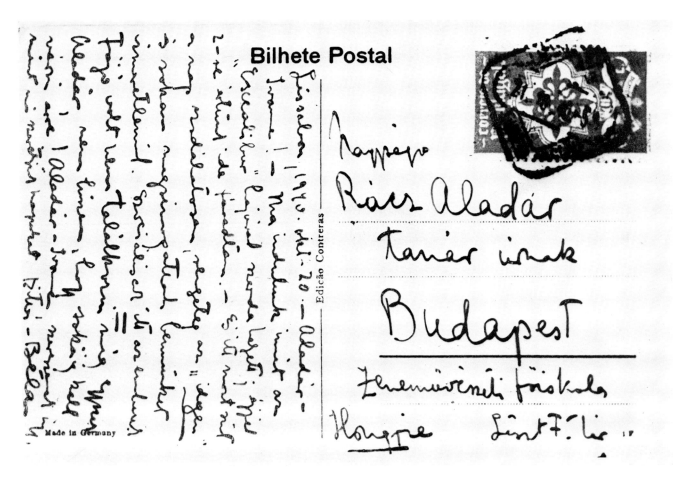

340 PERHAPS THE LAST MESSAGE SENT BY THE BARTÓKS FROM EUROPE

Mrs. Bartók's postcard to the great artist of the *cimbalom*, Aladár Rácz, and his wife.

"Lisbon, October 20, 1940.
Aladár—Ivonne,
Instead of Wednesday we are leaving here today by the 'Escalibur'; we arrived here at 2 a.m. dead beat. And here the sun is shining fabulously, there are lots of 'foreigners' here and many unknown people have patted our shoulders. Here people are social. It was painful not to have met you once more, Aladár; I don't think we'll have to wait for another meeting for a very long time! Aladár—Ivonne, do love us as much as we love you.

Ditta—Béla"

222

341–343 On board the S.S. "Escalibur", getting farther and farther from European shores

(Photos by Béla and Ditta Bartók)

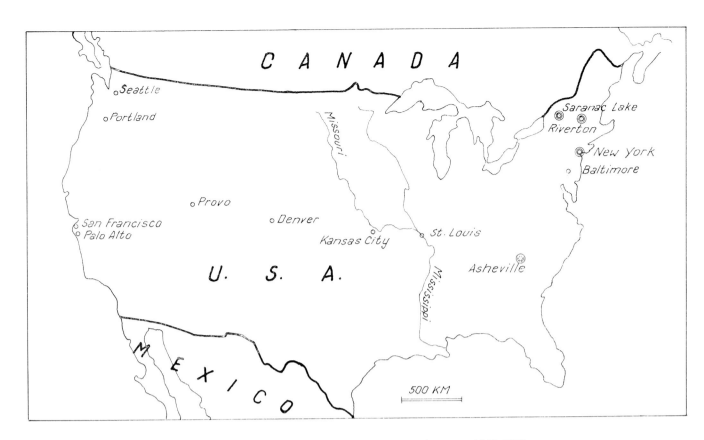

344 Map of Bartók's life and activity in America, 1940–1945

(Big circles indicate residences, small circles mark concert and lecture tours.)

345 FROM THE FIRST MONTH'S CONCERTS IN AMERICA

A two-piano recital in the New York Town Hall, November 24, 1940,

(Photo by John Albok)

Dr. Paul Hazard, dr. Karl T. Compton, Nicholas Murray Butler, President of Columbia University, Sir Cecil Thomas Carr and Bartók. November 25, 1940.

346 HONORARY DOCTOR OF COLUMBIA UNIVERSITY

347 WITH THE PARTICIPANTS IN THE 18TH CONGRESS OF THE INTERNATIONAL SOCIETY FOR CONTEMPORARY MUSIC

Second row, fourth from the right: Ernst Křenek; *top row, far right:* Bohuslav Martinů, with Benjamin Britten to his left. New York, May 1941.

348 3242, Cambridge Avenue, The Bronx, New York

Bartók's home from May 1941 to 1943.

(Copyright by G. D. Hackett)

349 A walk in New York, reminiscent of Buda

Along Bartók's route to Columbia University, where he worked at arranging systematically the collection of Serbo-Croatian folk music recorded by Milman Parry in 1941–1942.

(Copyright G. D. Hackett)

(The snapshots were taken by Dr. Alexander Honig, one of Bartók's doctors in America.)

(Photos by Dr. Alexander Honig)

354 With conductor Fritz Reiner, the eminent interpreter of his works in Westport, Connecticut

Reiner's name is associated with the world première held in New York on January 21, 1943, of the *Concerto* for two pianos, percussion and orchestra—transcribed from the *Sonata for Two Pianos and Percussion*. Spring 1942.

(Photo by Fritz Reiner)

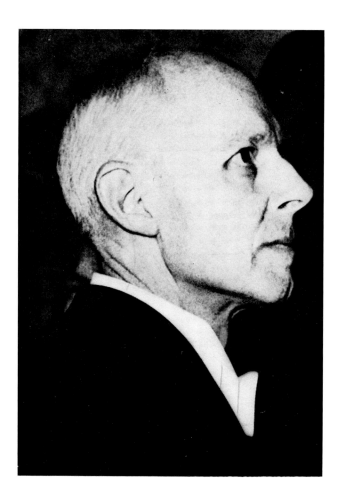

355–356 At what was perhaps the last concert...

May 4, 1943

Mr. Bela Bartok
3242 Cambridge Street
Riverdale
The Bronx, N.Y.

Dear Mr. Bartok:

It gives me great pleasure to inform you that
The Koussevitzky Music Foundation, Inc. has authorized
a grant to you of $1,000, to be offered to you with the
understanding that you will write a composition for orchestra. In connection with such grants the Foundation
requests that the composition be dedicated to the memory of Natalie Koussevitzky and that the manuscript, after
it is no longer needed for publication purposes, be depo-
sited with the Foundation.

This grant will be payable as follows: $500 on
receipt of your acceptance of the award, and $500 upon
the completion of the manuscript.

I look forward to an opportunity to talk this
matter over with you in the near future.

With best wishes.

Sincerely yours,

Serge Koussevitzky

265 Goddard Avenue
Brookline, Mass.

From November 1939 to the summer of 1943
Bartók did not write a single new work. In
the spring of 1943 the conductor Serge
Koussevitzky quite unexpectedly called on
him and commissioned him to write an
orchestral work.

Bartók, seriously ill, had considered his career
as composer practically finished, but this
commission stimulated him with new vigour.
Within fifty-five days he composed one of his
last great works: the *Concerto for Orchestra*.

358 32 Park Avenue,
Saranac Lake, N.Y.

*(Copyright
G. D. Hackett)*

It was in this house that
Bartók composed his
Concerto for Orchestra
between the 15th of
August and the 8th of
October, 1943. "Perhaps
as a result of better
health, I was able to
write a new orchestral
work," he reported with
his usual objectivity to
Mrs. Creel, his admirer
and former pupil, on the
creation of his new work.

359 Quite wasted ... nothing but skin and bones ... among trees and flowers, Summer 1943

(Copyright G. D. Hackett)

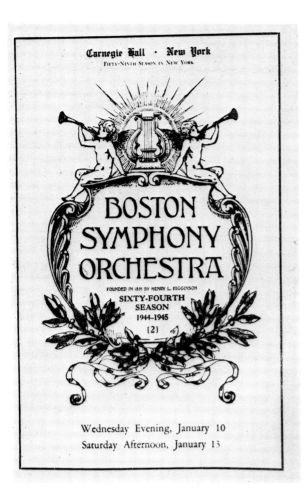

Carnegie Hall · New York
FIFTY-NINTH SEASON IN NEW YORK

Boston Symphony Orchestra

SERGE KOUSSEVITZKY, Conductor

SECOND EVENING CONCERT

WEDNESDAY, January 10

Programme

MOUSSORGSKY.........................Prelude to "Khovanstchina"

BARTÓK.........................Concerto for Orchestra
    I.   Andante non troppo; allegro vivace
    II.   Allegro scherzando
    III.   Elegy: Andante non troppo
    IV.   Intermezzo interrotto: Allegretto
    V.   Finale: Presto
             (First performance in New York)

INTERMISSION

BRAHMS.........................Symphony No. 1 in C minor, Op. 68
    I.   Un poco sostenuto: Allegro
    II.   Andante sostenuto
    III.   Un poco allegretto e grazioso
    IV.   Adagio; Allegro non troppo, ma con brio

BALDWIN PIANO

The music of these programmes is available at the Music Library,
58th Street Branch, The New York Public Library.

[3]

"Koussevitzky is very enthusiastic about the piece, and says it is 'the best orchestra piece of the last 25 years' (including the works of his idol Shostakovich!). At least, this is his personal opinion."

(Bartók to Mrs. Wilhelmine Creel, December 17, 1944)

The composer and conductor Tibor Serly belonged to Bartók's "inner circle" during his years in America. After Bartók's death he orchestrated the last 17 bars of the *Concerto No. 3* for piano and orchestra and he "deciphered" the short-hand sketches of the unfinished *Concerto* for viola and orchestra as well.

363 "FROM HEAVEN THE ANGELS DESCENDED..."

At the time when the Allied Forces landed in France, Bartók drew this sketch along with the first bars of a well-known Christmas carol. 1944.

364 Bartók's last home: 309 West 57th Street, New York 19, N.Y.

(Copyright G. D. Hackett)

Bartók in his New York home on 57th Street, with his pupil Ann Chenee.

(Copyright G. D. Hackett)

The *Concerto No. 3* for piano and orchestra was first performed after Bartók's death. Its world première was held in Philadelphia on January 27, 1946, with Gyorgy Sándor as soloist under the baton of Eugene Ormandy.

367 THE COMPOSER, SERIOUSLY ILL, AT HIS PIANO   *(Photo Newsweek)*

368 THE LAST SNAPSHOTS OF BARTÓK'S HANDS PLAYING THE PIANO

(Photos by Tibor Serly)

369 IN NEW YORK, JULY 5, 1944   *(Photo by Joseph Zwilich)*

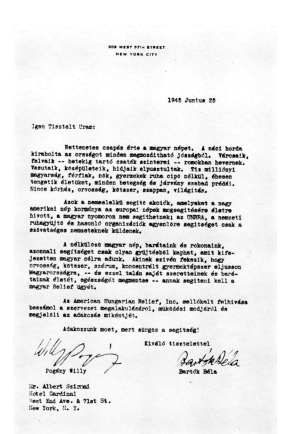

370 ONE OF THE LAST LETTERS

Three months before he died, Bartók asked for assistance for the Hungarian people, who had suffered so much during the war.

371 DRAFT OF THE "CONCERTO" FOR VIOLA AND ORCHESTRA, WHICH REMAINED UNFINISHED

372 West Side Hospital, New York   *(Copyright G. D. Hackett)*

"...And yet, I, too, would like to return (to Hungary), for good ——"
Bartók wrote in one of his last letters. He was not to realize his ambition:
his body was finally defeated by the fatal disease leukemia. Shortly before
noon on September 26, 1945, Bartók died in the hospital on the corner of
Sixth Avenue and 57th Street.

BARTOK—Bela, on Wednesday, Sept. 26, beloved husband of Edith Bartok, father of Bela and Peter Bartok. Services at "The Universal Chapel," Lexington Ave., at 52d St., on Friday, Sept. 28, at 2 P. M.

BARTOK—Bela. We announce with profound sorrow the death of the distinguished composer, Bela Bartok, in New York on Sept. 26, 1945.

DEEMS TAYLOR, President.
American Society of Composers,
Authors and Publishers.

373–374

375

APPENDIX

The following index indicates those members of Bartók's family and such of his contemporaries as either played a role in the composer's life and are mentioned in this volume's biographical introduction or pictorial documents. Numerals in regular type face (page number) refer to those mentioned in the biographical, numerals in bold (number of picture) those in the pictorial part. We include in the index significant contemporaries figuring in the pictorial part and those whose connection with Bartók is documented by the facsimile of an original manuscript.

248

Bartók, Béla Jr. (b. 1910) the composer's elder son

Bartók, Mrs. Béla, Ditta Pásztory (b. 1903) the composer's second wife (from 1923). She had been Bartók's pupil and, from 1938, his partner in their two-piano recitals. Together they performed the *Sonata for Two Pianos and Percussion* for the first time (1938), as well as its transcription with orchestral accompaniment (1943), and that for two pianos of *Mikrokosmos* (1940). It was for her that Bartók wrote his last Composition, the *Concerto No. 3* for piano and orchestra

Bartók, Mrs. Béla, Paula Voit (1857–1939) the composer's mother

Bartók, Mrs. Béla, Márta Ziegler (1893–1967) the composer's first wife (1909–1923)

Bartók, Erzsébet (Elza), Mrs. Emil Oláh-Tóth (1885–1955) the composer's sister

Bartók, János (1817–1877) the composer's grandfather

Bartók, Péter (b. 1924) the composer's younger son

Basilides, Mária (1886–1946) opera and concert-singer (contralto). Life member of the Budapest Opera House, an ardent propagator of Bartók's and Kodály's works. She sang the première of the

song cycle *Village Scenes* (in 1926), of sixteen of the *Twenty Hungarian Folk-Songs* in (1930) and of the *Five Hungarian Folk-Songs* with orchestral accompaniment (in 1933)
19, **206, 269**

Berg, Alban (1885–1935)
    Lyric Suite   20
    Violin Concerto   20

Beu, Octavian (1903–1964) Rumanian writer on musical subjects. In 1930 he wrote a paper on those of Bartók's compositions which have Rumanian connections. Though never published, thanks to correspodence about this paper, numerous important ideas of Bartók's about his own works have survived
23, **225**

Bianu, Ion (1856–1935) librarian of the Rumanian Academy of Sciences
15–16

Brăiloiu, Constantin (1893–1958) eminent Rumanian researcher of folk music
304

Britten, Benjamin (b. 1913)
347

Bușiția, Ion (1876–1953) drawing master of the Belényes (now Beiuş, Rumania) grammar-school. He helped Bartók very much in preparing his tours for collecting Rumanian folk-songs. Bartók dedicated his *Rumanian Folk Dances* to him
16, 18, **147**

Busoni, Ferruccio (1866–1924) composer and pianist
19

Čapek, Karel (1890–1938) the famous Czech writer
228–229

Casals, Pablo (b. 1876)
19, **199**

Chenee, Ann American piano teacher, Bartók's pupil in New York
365

Creel, Wilhelmine (-Driver) American pianist and scholar of oriental languages. In 1936–1937 she studied the piano under Bartók in Budapest. Bartók addressed numerous important letters to her during his years in America
25, **358**

Debussy, Claude Achille (1862–1918)
13, 14, 15, 19
    Pelléas and Mélisande 15

Delius, Frederick (1862–1934) English composer. He first met Bartók in 1910. Bartók wrote several important letters to him
19

250

Dille, Denijs (b. 1904) Belgian musicologist, from 1961 to 1971 head of the Bartók Archives of the Hungarian Academy of Sciences. He prepared for the press numerous compositions and scholarly works of Bartók's. Since the publication of his first book on Bartók in 1938, his biographical research has been of fundamental importance in the literature on the composer
19, 25, 260

Dohnányi, Ernst von (1877–1960) pianist and composer, from 1919 President-Conductor of the Budapest Philharmonic Society. He conducted the premières of the *Four Orchestral Pieces* in 1922 and of the *Dance Saite* in 1923
17, 18, 22, **167, 213–215, 275**

Durigo, Ilona (1881–1943) eminent Hungarian mezzosoprano
19

Erkel, László (1844–1896), Bartók's piano teacher in Pozsony in the school-year 1892/93 and from the autumn of 1894 to 1896
11, 22, **18**

Fábián, Felicitas (1884–1908) pupil of Thomán and Koessler at the Budapest Academy of Music. One of Bartók's idols in his youth
31

Failoni, Sergio (1890–1948) Italian conductor. From 1928 up to his death he was engaged by the Budapest Opera House. In 1936 he conducted the revival of *Bluebeard's Castle* at the Opera House
19, **216, 280, 298**

Fassett, Agatha American writer of Hungarian origin. The book she wrote on Bartók's years in America is mostly made up of personal experiences
13, **350–351**

Ferencsik, János (b. 1907) conductor. He conducted Bartók's last concert in Budapest, also his last concert in Europe on October 8, 1940
19, **338, 339**

Furtwängler, Wilhelm (1886–1954) renowned German conductor. He conducted the world première of Bartók's *Concerto No. 1* for piano and orchestra in Frankfurt am Main in 1927, at which the composer was soloist
18

Gaál, Mózes (1863–1936) writer, Bartók's form-master at the Pozsony grammar-school
247

Gertler, André (b. 1907) violinist, frequently Bartók's partner in chamber-music performances in the 1930s. In 1931 he transcribed Bartók's *Sonatina*, originally composed for the piano, for violin and piano
18, 260, **299, 311**

Geyer, Stefi (1888–1956) violinist. In 1907–1908 Bartók composed for her his *Violin Concerto* (No. 1)
14, 18, **73**

Goodman, Benny (b. 1909) American jazz-clarinetist. It was he who commissioned Bartók to write *Contrasts*, which Bartók dedicated to him and to Szigeti
19, **334–335**

Gruber, Mrs. Henrik, Emma Sándor (see *Kodály, Mrs. Zoltán, Emma Sándor*)

Haselbeck, Olga (1888–1961) opera singer (soprano). Life member of the Budapest Opera House. The first Judith of Bartók's *Bluebeard's Castle*
144–146

Hawkes, Ralph (1898–1950) London music publisher, one of the heads of the firm Boosey & Hawkes
26

Herz, Otto (b. 1894) pianist and famous accompanist. Has been living in the United States since 1939. Between the two world wars he assisted at numerous concerts of Bartók and Kodály in Hungary
18, 260, **213–214, 216, 322**

Hindemith, Paul (1895–1963)
234, 235

Hornbostel, Erich Moritz von (1877–1935) Austrian musicologist, a pioneer of comparative musicology
235

Hubay, Jenő (1858–1937) violinist, teacher and composer. From 1919 to 1934 Director of the Budapest Academy of Music. In 1904 he played at its première Bartók's early *Sonata* for violin and piano, with the composer at the piano. In 1909 he conducted the first complete performance of *Suite No. 1*. Later their relationship became strained
18

Jemnitz, Alexander (1890–1963) music critic and composer
298

József, Attila (1905–1937) poet, Bartók's contemporary, though twenty-four years his junior. As co-editor of the Budapest periodical *Szép Szó*, he published several of Bartók's writings. Among his posthumous papers the draft of a study on Bartók was found
23

Kacsóh, Pongrác (1873–1923) composer. His most popular work is the musical play *János vitéz* (Hero John). He was one of the first to discover Bartók's talent and to propagate his work
32

Kálmán, Oszkár (1887–1971) opera singer (bass). Life member of the Budapest Opera House. He was the first to sing the name part of Bartók's opera
144–146

Kecskeméti, Pál (b. 1901) and his wife, the harpsichordist Erzsébet Láng, belonged to the circle of Bartók's closest friends in the last three years of the composer's life. It was for him that Bartók composed the arrangement of the Ukranian folk-song *The Husband's Lament*
25

Kerner, István (1867–1929) conductor. Between 1900–1904 and then between 1916–1919 he was first conductor, and then between 1904–1913 President-Conductor, of the Budapest Philharmonic Society, whose Honorary President he remained from 1919 to his death. The première of Bartók's symphonic poem *Kossuth* was conducted by him in 1904
54

Kerpely, Jenő (1885–1954) violincellist, founder member of the Waldbauer–Kerpely String Quartet. He was active in the premières of numerous compositions by Bartók
18, 19, **101, 264**

Mengelberg, Willem (1871–1951) Dutch conductor, He conducted in 1938 the première of Bartók's great *Violin Concerto* with Zoltán Székely as soloist
18

Menuhin, Yehudi (b. 1916) American violinist. He gave the first performance of Bartók's *Sonata for Solo Violin* in 1944, a work the composer wrote at his request
19, 26

Mihalovich, Ödön (1842–1929) composer; Director of the Budapest Academy of Music (1887–1919) the successor of Liszt and Erkel
25

Molnár, Antal (b. 1890) musicologist, pioneer in the aesthetics and sociology of music in Hungary, author of the first analysis of Bartók and of the first book on Kodály
8, 9, 14, 18, 19, **101**

Müller-Widmann, Annie (1893–1964) wife of Dr. Oscar Müller, Prof. of Dentistry in Basel. Bartók wrote numerous important letters to her
24, 260, **325**

Nádasdy, Kálmán (b. 1904) opera director, translator, Director of the State Opera House of Budapest between 1959 and 1966. He produced the Budapest revival of *Bluebeard's Castle*, in 1936
260, **280**

Némethy, Ella (1895–1961) opera singer (dramatic soprano). Life member of the Budapest Opera House. At the 1936 Budapest revival of *Bluebeard's Castle* she sang the role of Judith
280

Norlind, Tobias (1879–1947) Swedish musicologist
249

Oláh, Gusztáv (1901–1956) opera director and designer. He designed the sets of the Budapest revival of *Bluebard's Castle* in 1936
280

Oláh-Tóth, Mrs. Emil (see *Bartók, Erzsébet*)

Ormandy, Eugene (b. 1899) American conductor of Hungarian origin. In 1946 he conducted the world première of Bartók's *Piano Concerto No. 3*
19

Primrose, William (b. 1903) Scottish soloist on the viola. It was at his request that Bartók wrote his *Concerto for Viola*, which remained unfinished
19, 26

Rácz, Aladár (1886–1958) soloist on the cimbalom, discovered by Ansermet and Stravinsky. He, on the other hand, "discovered" the cimbalom for the concert hall
316–317, 340

Reiner, Fritz (1888–1963) conductor of Hungarian origin, active in America. In Budapest he was a pupil of Thomán, Koessler and Bartók. The premières of numerous Bartók compositions in America are connected with his name (*Suites Nos. 1* and *2, Dance Suite, The Miraculous Mandarin Suite, Concerto No. 1* for piano and orchestra). In 1943 he conducted the world première of the *Concerto* for two pianos, percussion and orchestra with Bartók and his wife playing the piano parts
18, 260, **354**

Reinitz, Béla (1878–1943) composer of songs, music critic, Head of the Music Directorium of the 1919 Hungarian Republic of Councils. The first composer to put Ady's poems to music. Bartók dedicated to him his own Ady songs
17, **245**

Richter, Hans (1843–1916) conductor of Hungarian origin, active in Hungary, Austria, Germany and Britain. In 1876 he conducted the inaugurating performances of the Bayreuth Festspielhaus. In 1904 he conducted in Manchester the English première of Bartók's symphonic poem *Kossuth*
11, **49, 57**

Rosbaud, Hans (1895–1962) German conductor. He conducted the world première of Bartók's *Concerto No. 2* for piano and orchestra in Frankfurt am Main, on the 23rd January 1933
242

Roth, Fery (1899–1969) violinist, leader of the Roth Quartet
19, **331**

Sacher, Paul (b. 1906) Swiss conductor, founder of the Basel Chamber Orchestra. He commissioned Bartók to compose his *Music for String Instruments, Percussion and Celesta* and his *Divertimento* for string orchestra. Sacher conducted the premières of these two works (1937, 1940) as also the world première of Bartók's *Violin Concerto No. 1* (1958)
19, 24, 260, **288–290**

Sándor, Gyorgy (b. 1912) pianist, the first soloist in Bartók's *Concerto No. 3* for piano and orchestra in 1946
19, 260, **366**

Saygun, A. Adnan (b. 1907) professor of the Conservatoire of Istanbul, Turkish composer and folk-music researcher, Bartók's collaborator during his folk-music collecting tour of Turkey in 1936
281, 284

Schoenberg, Arnold (1874–1951)
19, 20, 21, **113–114**
    Harmonielehre 19, **113–114**
    String Quartet No. 1, op. 7, 19
    Three Pieces for Piano, op. 11, 19

Selden-Goth, Gisela (b. 1884) composer and writer on music, she studied composition under Bartók in the first decade of the century
87

Serly, Tibor (b. 1900) American composer and conductor of Hungarian origin. He completed the score of Bartók's *Concerto No. 3* for piano and orchestra, and he "broke the code" of the sketches of the *Concerto* for viola and orchestra which he wrote down
19, 25, 26, 260, **362**

Strasser, István (b. 1889) conductor. He conducted the first performance in Vienna of Bartók's *Concerto No. 1* for piano and orchestra in 1927 with the composer as soloist
18, 20

Strauss, Richard (1864–1949)
11, **13**, 19
    Thus Spake Zoroaster 11

Szabolcsi, Bence (b. 1899) creator of modern Hungarian music history. Kodály's pupil, Bartók's and Kodály's collaborator, and author of the first Hungarian scholarly biography of Bartók (1955)
8, 23, 259

Székely. Mihály (1901–1963) opera singer (bass). Life member of the Budapest Opera House. At the Budapest revival in 1936 of *Bluebeard's Castle* he sang the name part of the opera. His interpretation of Bluebeard has been recorded twice
280

Székely, Zoltán (b. 1903) violinist. From 1937 leader of the Hungarian String Quartet; Bartók's chamber-music partner in the 1920s and 1930s. Bartók dedicated to him his *Rhapsody No. 2* (1928) and his *Violin Concerto* (No. 2, 1937–38). Székely performed the former in the year it was created (its variant with orchestra in 1932) and the latter in 1939. He transcribed Bartók's *Rumanian Folk Dances* for violin and piano
18, 260, **178–179**

Székelyhidy, Ferenc (1885–1954) opera and concert singer (tenor). Life member of the Budapest Opera House. He rendered great service in the popularization of Hungarian folk-songs. At the première of Kodály's *Psalmus Hungaricus* he sang the tenor part
19, **213–214, 216**

Szenkár, Eugene (b. 1891) conductor. In 1926 he conducted in Cologne the world première of *The Miraculous Mandarin*
18

Szigeti, Joseph (b. 1892) violinist, Bartók's chamber-music partner from the 1920s to 1940. The *Rhapsody No. 1* is dedicated to him—*Contrasts* to Szigeti and to Benny Goodman
18, 25, 260, **190, 191, 219, 267, 268, 332–335**

Takács, Jenő (b. 1902) Hungarian composer and pianist living in Austria
260, **234–235**

Talich, Václav (1883–1961) Czech conductor
18

Tango, Egisto (1873–1951) Italian conductor, active at the Budapest Opera House between 1912 and 1919. He conducted the premières of *The Wooden Prince* (1917) and *Bluebeard's Castle* (1918), the first being dedicated to him
17, 18, **141**

Taylor, Deems (b. 1885) American composer. As President of ASCAP he did much to assist Bartók in recovering his health (1943–1945)
25

Temesváry, János (1891–1964) violinist, Professor of the Academy of Music, second violinist of the first Waldbauer–Kerpely String Quartet
101

Thomán, István (1862–1941) pianist and teacher; a former pupil of Liszt; Bartók's piano teacher at the Budapest Academy of Music (1899–1903). Bartók dedicated to him his piano composition *Study for the Left Hand* (1903)
10, **29, 31, 305**

Toscanini, Arturo (1867–1957)
23, **233**

Tóth, Aladár (1898–1968) music aesthetician, the most significant music critic of the period between the two world wars. Militant adherent of Bartók's and Kodály's music. Director of the Budapest State Opera House between 1946 and 1956
14, **213, 298**

Valéry, Paul (1871–1945) French poet
229

Varèse, Edgar (1883–1965) French composer, lived from 1915 in the United States. He was the first to conduct there one of Bartók's compositions for orchestra: *Two Pictures*
18

Vásárhelyi, Zoltán (b. 1900) renowned Hungarian choral conductor. The first performances of several choral works by Bartók and Kodály took place under his baton
298

Vecsey, Ferenc (1893–1935) violinist
61

Végh, Sándor (b. 1912) violinist and string-quartet leader
276

Voit, Irma (1849–1941) the "Aunt Irma" of Bartók's letters: his mother's sister
10, 17, **33, 37–38**

Waldbauer, Imre (1892–1952) violinist, founder and leader of the Waldbauer–Kerpely String Quartet. Bartók's *String Quartets Nos. 1* and *2* were first performed by this group. Waldbauer was often Bartók's partner in chamber music
18, 19, **101, 244–245 263–264**

Webern, Anton (1883–1945)
20

Wellesz, Egon (b. 1885) musicologist and composer of Austrian origin, now living in Britain
235

Zágon, Géza Vilmos (1890–1918) composer, musicologist, one of the propagators of the new trend in music in Hungary around 1910. He assisted Bartók in the preparation of his African tour in 1913. Died in an Italian Army Hospital in the First World War
15, **115–116**

Zathureczky, Ede (1903–1959) violinist, from the 1930s on often Bartók's partner in chamber music. General Director of the Budapest Academy of Music between 1943 and 1956. From 1957 up to his death he was Professor at Indiana University in Bloomington
19

EPILOGUE

It is not for the first time that the author has undertaken to depict Bartók's life and career by means of pictorial documents. He owes the idea of organizing an iconographical collection concerning Bartók to *Bence Szabolcsi*, author of the first Hungarian biography of Bartók of scholarly authenticity—as indeed he owes him so many other things. Szabolcsi's biography was first published in 1955 in the Budapest periodical *Csillag* (Star). *Béla Tardos*, the then director of Editio Musica, Budapest, wanted to publish this biography as an independent volume and included it in the series "Lives of Hungarian Composers in Pictures". At Professor Szabolcsi's request this publishing house commissioned the present writer to compile a second section of the volume: the series of pictures with accompanying commentary. The title-page of the small volume was the following: *Bartók Béla élete. Írta: Szabolcsi Bence. Bartók élete képekben. Összeállította: Bónis Ferenc* (The Life of Béla Bartók by Bence Szabolcsi. Bartók's Life in Pictures compiled by Ferenc Bónis). With an ever enlarged picture section the book went into three editions in Hungarian within a short time (1956 with 105 pictures, [2]/1958: 119 pictures, [3]/1961: 126 pictures). The revised and enlarged third Hungarian edition was the basis of the first edition in a foreign language—that in Russian—brought out in 1963 (Corvina Press, Budapest, 127 pictures). In 1964 three further editions in a larger format and with 264 pictures came out in English, French and German (the biographical introductions of the first two were written by Bence Szabolcsi, that of the third by the present writer). The volumes were brought out by Corvina Press (French version), by Corvina and Boosey & Hawkes Music Publishers Limited, London (English version) and by Corvina Press and Boosey & Hawkes GmbH., Bonn (German version).

The present volume differs from the above not only in its larger format but also in its richer pictorial material, amounting to 375 illustrations. The sixteen years spent in compiling it enabled us to select the most characteristic pictorial documents, and in particular those which have survived in the best state of preservation. It also made possible more accurate commentary on the pictures and opportunity of satisfying scholarly interests without disappointing the reader simply interested in Bartók's life and work. A further possible continuation of this book will strive in all respects to meet scholarly standards: with a pictorial documentation of the various phases of the biography, of contemporaries and last but not least of the works themselves in as complete a sense as possible. Of course, completeness approximates to exactitude.

To produce a work of this kind depends on three main conditions: the publisher's enterprising spirit; the acknowledging of the principle that with this kind of documentary work it is the material that determines the size of the volume and not the other way round; and most important the thoroughgoing support of readers, individuals and institutions. We can fulfil our task only if we are able to rely, as in the past, upon the owners or custodians of pictures and documents giving us permission to publish them, and further assisting our work with their advice, guidance and the passing on of information that perhaps only they may know of.

It is the author's pleasant duty to express here his gratitude to all who have helped him until now. First of all to Professor *Bence Szabolcsi*, who, as already mentioned, was the initiator of this book and who contributed personal memories; but particularly because from the beginning he has followed our work with interest and furthered it with his advice. It is with gratitude that we remember *Zoltán Kodály:* his guidance alone was more precious than the documentary material he put at our disposal. *Mrs. Károly Ziegler, née Márta Ziegler*, Bartók's first wife, was particularly helpful in locating and dating photographs taken in the 1910s. This volume has been enriched with much valuable information by *Mrs. Béla Bartók, Ditta Pásztory*, the composer's widow, who also permitted the publication of numerous rare and precious pictures. The special "Bartók maps" of the volume have been executed by technical counsellor of the Hungarian State Railways, engineer *Béla Bartók Jr.* He made possible publication of a number of pictures and read with meticulous care worthy of his father, the volume in manuscript. Our work has been assisted by Professor *Denijs Dille*, with unselfish zeal. He put rare and valuable pictures at our disposal, and facilitated the systematizing of our material by means of the rich range of data contained in his scholarly publications. *János Demény*'s uniquely detailed biographical documentation and critical comments allowed us to date and identify some of the pictures. (Quotations in the text from letters written by Bartók correspond to [*Béla Bartók Letters*. Collected, selected, edited and annotated by János Demény, Corvina–Faber and Faber, Budapest–London, 1971]). Among Bartók's pupils and close adherents *Mme. Annie Müller-Widmann, Mrs. Mária Popper-Lukács, Mrs. Etelka Milroy-Freund, Mrs. Irma Hercz-Freund and Mrs. Irén Révész-Egry* filled out the portrait of the man and the artist with valuable pictures and reminiscences. For numerous pictorial documents of the years in America we are indebted to the co-operation of *Dr. Albert Sirmay, Dr. Alexander Honig,* and *Joseph Zwilich.* Bartók's colleagues in the field of music—such as *Ernest Ansermet, André Gertler, Dr. Otto Herz, Antal Molnár, Kálmán Nádasdy, Dr. Fritz Reiner, Dr. Paul Sacher, Gyorgy Sándor, Tibor Serly, Zoltán Székely and his wife* as well as *Joseph Szigeti*—also contributed to this volume with pictures or with reminiscences. The painter *Valerie Wolffenstein* put at our disposal her drawing of Bartók (signed by him), and the music critic *Dr. Jenő Antal Molnár* permitted us to publish valuable snapshots. For pictures, reminiscences and advice in plenty we are indebted to *Mme. Yvonne Rácz,* widow of the cimbalom artist Aladár Rácz, to *Imre Kun,* who used to be Bartók's concert manager, the physician *Dr. Renée Bátor, David Clegg, Mme. Nelly Failoni,* the widow of the conductor Sergio Failoni, the conductor *Jenő Kenessey, Gyula Kertész, Mme. Aya Petzold,* the daughter of Mme. Annie Müller-Widmann, Professor *Jenő Takács, Lajos Voit,* Bartók's cousin, *Mrs. Pál Voit,* Bartók's niece and to her daughter *Dr. Krisztina Voit.* In collecting material from Vienna *Peter Riethus* provided assistance, as did *László Somfai* in respect of the Budapest material. We also express our thanks to the various photographers—*Károly Escher, Kata Kálmán, Alex Kertész, József Pécsi* and *Dénes Rónai*—who put at our disposal their photographs of Bartók. In taking photographs of American locations the New York photographer *G. D. Hackett* was of assistance. We wish also to acknowledge the kind assistance of the following institutions: the *Bartók Archives of the Institute of Musicology of the Hungarian Academy of Sciences* (Budapest), the *Liszt Ferenc Academy of Music* (Budapest), the *Budapest Philharmonic Society,* the *Hungarian State Opera House* (Budapest), the *Institute for the Labour Movement* (Budapest), the *Budapest Museum of History* and the *National Széchényi Library* (Budapest). The reproduction of scores in manuscript or printed form was kindly permitted by *Boosey & Hawkes Ltd.* (London), by *Universal Edition A. G.* (Vienna), and by *Editio Musica Budapest.* Finally thanks are also due to the expertise and patience of the editorial and technical staff of Editio Musica Budapest and of Corvina Press.

Many people who selflessly helped during the compilation of the pictorial documentation did not live to see the completion of this book. Here too we pay tribute to their memory, by making public property all the documents that throw light upon Bartók's place in the life and art of our century. We request our readers kindly to assist in this continuing endeavour in the future.

Ferenc Bónis